Our Beguine

THE DANCE OF LIFE

JOEL M. LEVIN, MD

authorHOUSE®

AuthorHouse™
1663 Liberty Drive
Bloomington, IN 47403
www.authorhouse.com
Phone: 1-800-839-8640

Published by AuthorHouse   03/06/2015

ISBN: 978-1-4969-5947-8 (sc)
ISBN: 978-1-4969-5948-5 (hc)
ISBN: 978-1-4969-5946-1 (e)

Library of Congress Control Number: 2014922348

Print information available on the last page.

Any people depicted in stock imagery provided by Thinkstock are models, and such images are being used for illustrative purposes only. Certain stock imagery © Thinkstock.

This book is printed on acid-free paper.

Because of the dynamic nature of the Internet, any web addresses or links contained in this book may have changed since publication and may no longer be valid. The views expressed in this work are solely those of the author and do not necessarily reflect the views of the publisher, and the publisher hereby disclaims any responsibility for them.

Scripture quotations marked KJV are from the Holy Bible, King James Version (Authorized Version). First published in 1611. Quoted from the KJV Classic Reference Bible, Copyright © 1983 by The Zondervan Corporation.

Mona Lisa, Mona Lisa, men have named you
You're so like the lady with the mystic smile
Is it only cause you're lonely they have blamed you?
For that Mona Lisa strangeness in your smile?

—written by Ray Evans and Jay Livingston

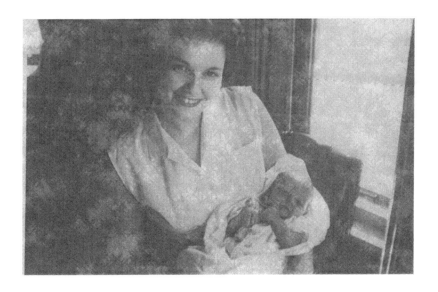

To Donna with everlasting love

A good wife who can find? She is far more precious than jewels.

—Proverbs 31:10–31

Contents

Part 1

The Story before Donna

Part 2

At Last The Real Dance Begins

Acknowledgments

Of course, my sincerest thanks go to the many talented songwriters and lyricists whose music Donna and I loved, as do so many of our generation and the younger people who have followed us into this life. I give the composers and lyricists great credit for their ability to capture the emotions of life through their beautiful words and music. Other than my personal thoughts in prose and poetry, I am acknowledging that it is their work that inspired me and will undoubtedly belong to the ages. I owe them a great deal of gratitude for soothing my feelings as I write this memoir and humbly ask permission to showcase their wonderful music and lyrics in a small and respectful manner.

I thank our dear parents for bringing us into the world, interestingly at the same time and in the same area. Was that a higher energy or source at work? I shall never know. Were we traveling souls from the very start, destined to share our current life together? As to travels, we are grateful to our grandparents who traveled far across the world to bring us to this great and glorious nation, create our American clan, and share in the American dream. And share Donna and I did. Dad had a favorite saying about traveling through life with Mom. He always expressed the feeling that they would stem the tide of life together. How profound and clear that emotion is to me today.

To my friends who have walked with Donna and me along the road we mutually shared, I send my everlasting love. To my soul mate, it is too late to physically communicate with her, but through my heart and with all my soul, I have dedicated this memoir to memorialize and capture our life's journey.

I wish to thank the publishers, coordinators, and editors of AuthorHouse for helping me develop this work as well as the many friends and family who contributed knowingly or unknowingly in helping me reconstruct our dance of life.

Preface

This is a memory trail (a memoir so to speak) about my lifetime journey with my dear wife, Donna, who died May 11, 2013. Her passing left me with a feeling of emptiness, as if part of me had been torn away. How persistent and pernicious this feeling has turned out to be to this very day and this very moment. I have a strong desire and, before my memory fails me, an urgent need to memorialize her. What better manner can there be than by telling our story to you and once again reminding myself of the road I traveled with a lovely lady?

Alfred, Lord Tennyson, wrote, "'Tis better to have loved and lost than never to have loved at all." However, he did not comment on the ongoing love that remains when death does us part. They say that true love is when two people bond together in happiness and dedication, creating a singular kindred spirit. We, not I, became the whole of my life.

When Donna died, her passing left me with a feeling of emptiness, as if part of me had been torn away. I seek Donna everywhere and think about her constantly, and she remains deeply enshrined in my mind and my heart. This will be a key discussion later on as we begin to look at the concept of the soul as a separate and free entity when the physical part of life ends. Communication and trying to develop a newer relationship with my wife along our now different plains of existence has been difficult for me. Many stories relate to folks who have had their loved ones appear in a vision or a dream, telling them that all is all right. I did once have such an experience on the night my father died. It seemed real as he stood there before me and asked me to take care of my mother. Was it an illusion? I felt as if I were wide awake. But I have not seen Donna in such dreams or nighttime illusions. Yet I yearn to know that a part of her (be it atoms, molecules, subparticles, or an intact soul) still exists in this vast universe that we know so little of. For me, for now, it is grief, sorrow, loneliness, and of course the powerless feeling I carry inside as it clings to my very core.

I wrote this book because I wanted to capture within my yet alert mind all I remember about our life together; thus, this book is a memoir. It is also meant to remind those who walk with me, as I am not alone, of my gratitude to them. I wish to acknowledge them. And lastly, since this has been a wonderful outlet for my emotions, it is an attempt at recovery. Therefore, there are two parts to this memoir, one remembering a wonderful life with Donna and the other analyzing the more mysterious aspects of life and what follows beyond the physical existence.

Alas, I still had that empty feeling as I began this project, and in spite of what the song says, "I'll see you in my dreams," dreams do not work for me as I end each day and try to lapse into sleep. I have not had the good fortune to have visions or dreams of Donna happen to me.

As of this moment, I live in solitude and isolation, even in the midst of friends and my dear family. I live today but exist in yesterday because past memory and longing for yesterday remain a great part of my current existence. She was the music in my heart, the balm of my soul, and without any doubt, my soul mate during our *dance of life*. I will get to the use of this phrase in short order.

The question is often raised as to when life begins. You know the humor that surrounds this question as to when life begins and the theological arguments that more seriously address this. The thoughts run from the serious opinion (i.e., when there is a viable fetus) on to when the dog dies and the children have left home. None of these explanations satisfies me, and although once tickling my funny bone, I am sure that my beginning was when I met my wife. Incidentally, because of this unique bond, which becomes more apparent each and every day, I have no other wish for another life mate or companion, as many widows or widowers may have. Not me! I have had my one and only until death did us part.

Since I am the survivor, much as Elie Wiesel survived the death camps of Europe, there is, in a different sense, a commonality. It is as he has said, "Whoever survives a test, whatever it may be, must tell the story." It is my obligation to tell our story in the best fashion I can.

You can now ask why I chose a song title for this work I took on. The answer is that I am both a physician and a musician and songs help to lift my spirit up. I'll speak more about my career later on, but Donna was my partner in our dance of life.

Because music is so important, I knew it had to become part of how I told the story. The initial title for the memoir that I chose for this book was *Those Were the Days*, a song credited to Gene Raskin, who put English lyrics to a Russian romance song.

It is a wonderful song, and I have sung it many times, but I soon realized that I needed something more befitting, more substantial, an elegant description of the road we traveled and the journey we shared through our life together. As I have grown older and time surely escalates with each passing year, our fifty-seven years together now seem as if they were but a fleeting moment. There is that song "As Time Goes By," but that didn't seem to work either.

I searched my musical memory bank and eventually came upon "Our Beguine" as the title. It is based on the song "Begin the Beguine," written by Cole Porter (1891–1964) while on a cruise on Cunard's ocean liner.

A *beguine* was originally thought of as a Christian laywoman of the thirteenth or fourteenth century but evolved on to a mean a white woman and ultimately transformed itself to a dance and in particular, a slow couple's dance. It became popular in Parisian ballrooms because of the influence of the Cole Porter song. The words written by this great composer struck me immediately. The essential lyric that influenced me is as follows:

> To live it again is past all endeavor
> Except when the tune clutches my heart
> And there we are swearing to love forever
> And promising never to part …

The songs in my heart and embedded in my memory have stirred my emotions in taking on this not-so-small task of telling our story, and throughout the book, you will see references to lyrics that highlight the parts of the story I tell.

It is a memoir not written about a famous campaign or an important person. The intent is not to sum up our life as unique or of any great contribution to society; nor is it to serve as an older man's memoir or autobiography. It is my earnest attempt to keep my wife, Donna Joyce Krakow Levin, alive in my heart and in the minds of those who came to know her and may get to know her through reading this book. Again, it is to portray a soul-to-soul attachment, not define it, as that esoteric task is beyond me. I find that a memorial plaque in some institution, a charitable donation, or a good deed is not enough. I have done all of that. I must gift her with my memories so that all will get to know this gracious and valiant lady and once again stress the point that my life really began with her.

My life experience with Donna and, I hope, a newfound spirituality tells me that this union was meant to be. I think of it as our dance of life, which became the subtitle of this work. As you know, the rhythms of life change, the tempo sometimes fast and sometimes slow. As a musician, I feel that the daily sounds of life are sometimes discordant, sometimes mellow, but ever flowing onward like a brook or stream. To my musical self, it was indeed a dance during our time together on this plain of existence.

I hope that newfound friends, through choosing to read this book, will see the commonality in some of their experiences with their own loved ones. I wanted to make this book a passion for keeping a unique love journey alive but also to pepper the tale with memorable anecdotes and indeed some funny moments. Although our life's journey was never perfect and often a mixture of pleasure and problems, it was wonderful in a very special sense, the good fortune I had in marrying Donna. We will commence the tale defining my life before her and continue with my life with her and the period of my bereavement and soul searching after fifty-seven years of being together.

We had fifty-seven years of marriage together, hardly eternity but a long life together. As to forever or eternity, alas, this is not under our control. It is a phrase used in poetry and prose and is part of youthful thought processes; I used that term for many years but now understand it to be eternal love. "Till death do us part" as part of a marriage ceremony is certainly realistic, but is it completely true? I have not emotionally separated myself from her. I'm sure that many of you have started out in life with a partner you love and think that it will never end. The thought of death is not on your mind. As life goes on, those thoughts of eternity lead on to the pangs of reality when the physical being ends for the one you love and that separation issue (bereavement, mourning) takes hold. You can imagine how a part of you dies as well— mind you, not in body but in emotional turmoil due to this cruel act that God or physiology imposes upon us.

That certainly happened to me several years ago when Donna developed her first major illness in the year 2010. The reality of her ensuing long illness hit me like a ton of bricks, stopped me in my tracks, affected my concentration on my work, stilled my few pleasures, and ended my desire to create or play music as I had done up to that point. I did not realize that unknowingly I was going through the various phases of mourning, as theorized by Elizabeth Kübler-Ross in her 1969 dissertation at the University of Chicago and her 2005 book *On Death and Dying*. I had anger for some time, blaming others or myself for her demise. Did her doctors do something wrong, or was I to blame in some way?

I am at the realization stage right now but intuitively recognize that there needs be an additional stage beyond this. I guess some call it acceptance. Some also say time lightens the load. Tears help. Friends and relatives try. My loving daughter, Cheryl, and granddaughter, Sara, do their best by keeping the home fires burning and catering to my every need. Charitable offerings, purposefully upgrading our home with the intent of displaying all of Donna's collectibles, help remind me of her. This is still not enough, my grieving heart tells me! I have accepted her passing but still linger in the depths of my loss. There was a time when I could sit at the piano and create music that was right for the moment. It had always soothed me or given me pleasure. I remember the two musical pieces I played for my wife, "The Anniversary Waltz" and our life's theme song "Love Is a Many-Splendored Thing," the record that was on when she proposed to me. But now, age, arthritis, or some mysterious reason has robbed me of this escape. And so I searched and searched for another answer. I had written medical papers and put down my thoughts of the moment (some call it journaling), but this was to be different. It would have to be a major work, a summation of our life together. Was I up to the task? Would I succeed? I leave it to my readers to decide.

This brings me to this book I call *Our Beguine*. There is a certain joy that comes from recording our life together. There is no problem dragging me to this project, be it the first light of day or during night's quietude. My family sees me at work and perhaps in some measure shares in the sheer joy that I get in this my special undertaking. They see a certain period of my day as I concentrate on this project not seeming as depressed.

The book is designed to make it an interesting, easy-to-read memoir for those who chance to come upon it. It is not intended to be a self-help primer, a psychosocial treatise on life and death, or a program that one must follow. It simply is a step in making acceptance a reality for me and, with as yet a sound mind, a final step to give me a purpose as well as yielding a pinch of solace as I travel down memory lane. These days,

I have less need of food for sustenance (my daughter is concerned about that) than food for thought (which is my special need)!

I offer my sincerest gratitude to the many talented songwriters and lyricists, whose works are referenced within this memoir. Their music and lyrics, after I gave it some thought, became a method to capture those periods of life Donna and I went through. In a sense, it makes my humble offering more unique, I hope, capturing the interest of my contemporaries and introducing younger generations to some of the greatest American popular music. For me indeed, reexamination of the songs and lyrics I have known so well seems to be the gateway to keeping Donna alive in my heart. After all is said, she was the music of my heart …

It is a prime intention to make this book a passion for keeping a unique love journey alive but also to pepper the tale with memorable anecdotes and indeed some funny moments. There shall of course be remembrance about the troublesome travails that we humans all go through.

I wish to thank the publishers and editors of this work and the many friends and family who contributed knowingly or unknowingly in helping me reconstruct our dance of life.

It came to me after her passing that I needed to record our life's journey for our children as well to make this a heritage piece. It will give them a true look at who we were, not just as parents or family members, but as caring and—like all who inhabit this earth—fallible human beings.

It is time to tell the tale before life's next surprise befalls me.

This book, as I said, then has a multifocal pathway. Readers will come to understand this as they follow along with difficulty. It then delves into the seeking, searching, and meaning when we parted on this plain of existence. Marcel Proust said that memory nourishes the heart and grief abates. This then is my gift to her memory. I, in some way or manner, hold on to the feeling that in some manner or form we shall be together again. Perhaps that is what eternity means.

So please come along, even sing along, and share the music of our fifty-seven years together. It will not be difficult or heavy reading. It is sometimes sad, always sincere, and yet filled with lighthearted moments. To Donna, I dedicate this book and my eternal love. The embers burn on forever!

The Dance of Life

Life itself is a dance I say,
The tempo slow when life's anew.
It hastens with each passing day
With lessons learned and troubles few.

The dance of course starts out fast,
Yet skills of life are tough to learn.
Time goes on—the tempo fast.
For simpler days we sometimes yearn.

The babe becomes a younger man,
Moving on with each new beat.
Ambitions grow and quests begin.
What has yet to come; am I replete?

Of answers I was not aware
What destiny had in store for me.
This dance of life—with whom to share,
Oh no, my Beguine was yet to be.

Part 1

The Story before Donna

Not Yet Near My Shining Light

Chapter 1

● ●

Our Very Beginnings

My dear, I've a feeling you are
so near and yet so far
you appear like a radiant star
first so near then again so far.
—"So Near and Yet So Far" by Cole Porter

It was the best of times, it was the worst of times, it
was the age of wisdom, it was the age of foolishness, it
was the epoch of belief, it was the epoch of incredulity,
it was the season of Light, it was the season of Darkness,
it was the spring of hope, it was the winter of despair, we
had everything before us, we had nothing before us, we
were all going direct to Heaven, we were all going direct
the other way ... —Charles Dickens, *A Tale of Two Cities*

Charles Dickens and a *Tale of Two Cities* involved England and
France in the 1770s and our brave ancestors who dared to leave their
old homes for a new life. It was not my intent to minimize the work of

Charles Dickens. I just thought it would fit into the scheme of things to borrow the concept, as an analogy so to speak. The wisdom of this prose was a need to escape the bleakness of the Old World to other lands where streets were paved in gold. In a manner, it was the spring of hope.

Our tale was not a tale of two cities, but of one city and two youngsters who would come to know the best of times yet to come (and two moms, who were perhaps enduring the worst of times, during the Depression). It, as an analogy, depicts a tale of two mothers separated literally by a few miles of city streets while delivering their babies that night in April 1934. Two babies, unique to this story, were so close and yet so far. You could say that we were baby steps apart, yet years apart. That, to me, is incredible. It would be many years before Donna and I would reflect on this first interesting connection in our lives, and we would not even meet each other for many years. So it was not a tale of two cities but one city and two youngsters (and two moms, who were perhaps enduring the worst of times, as labor tends to go). For the moms, the pangs of labor are sometimes the worst of times. Please forgive this analogy; I am only a man who never experienced this kind of labor. I have labored in many ways but not in this physiological process. Vicariously, as a physician, I helped bring babies into the world. Would you believe that some moms honored me by naming their children after me?

To begin this tale, I have to start with my life story as I recall it. Each chapter will bring us closer to the start of my real life, when I met a wonderful lady who defined my life and captured my soul.

I was given the name Joel and the middle name of Merwin when I was born. What a moniker. And yes, my lifelong secret is out. I never gave out my middle name to anyone, as it had no meaning to me and seemed peculiar. Was my mother thinking of Merlin the magician or Merton, the boy who lived downstairs from us? She named me Joel because of her interest in the movie star Joel McCrea, but I don't know where the name Merwin came from. Of course, it was expected that I would carry the names of maternal and paternal heritage. That would be Vickar (maternal) and Le Vein (paternal). I changed the last name in grade school and became Joel M. Levin. My wife's name, Donna, means lady, and we all called her Bella Donna (a beautiful lady), as she was to everyone who knew her.

I grew up during the Depression years lacking for nothing in a household of parents, grandparents, and a few unmarried aunts. This was typical of many families in the 1930s. I had no knowledge of economic difficulty, as each member of the household contributed to the welfare of us all. I was oblivious to the motion and fast pace of people in and out of the house from dawn to well beyond dusk, working and sometimes enjoying some time away from our confined world. The baby Joel was assuredly content in his crib and was always the center of attention. This was my own little world.

That was until I developed asthma at a very early age. It is hereditary in my family, but living in a crowded apartment with a bunch of smokers certainly didn't help. I had many an asthmatic attack in those early days, and the medications in use today were not available then. Chicken soup, as a remedy, helped, and when the attack abated, the comic books my dad brought home helped me forget those episodes when I struggled with my breathing. It was super dad bringing me Superman.

The patriarch, my grandfather, was a journalist and a scholar, who took an early retirement because of a heart attack and what was called hardening of the arteries. Who at that time knew about cholesterol, gluten, fat, and all the modern stuff regarding healthy lifestyles and prevention of illness? We only knew that we ate what we ate, never bothered by warnings on labels or blood tests for everything. We only knew and were thankful that if it tasted good, it must be good.

I learned to play chess with my grandfather and did so until I was able to beat him. He then seemed to lose interest. I also remember that he was very religious but never pushed it on us. We were free to make our own choices.

One amusing anecdote about Grandpa goes like this. We had an old-fashioned telephone in our house, which required a slug equal to a nickel to make a call. A collector would come by regularly, determining how much was owed by the number of slugs. About the time I was growing up, the telephone company switched from a real operator to an automated one. I remember him listening to one of those early messages, swearing under his breath, and saying, "Madam, shut up and give me a chance to speak."

My grandmother was the love of my life, and as I grew up, we did many things together. She was the matriarch and handled the role as well as any queen might do. She had things under control (all under her thumb), argued well, and usually won all battles with the king of his castle (grandfather) with diplomacy but at times with an iron hand. Margaret Thatcher might have been related to her or it seems a kindred spirit to my grandmother. But as long as I was the prince in the palace, I was quite happy with her (her loving hand and her wondrous creations in our tiny kitchen). As to supplying the kitchen, we would walk to the nearest shopping area on Roosevelt Road in Chicago. We would make several stops, including, as I recall, two of the smelliest places on earth: the fish store and the butcher's. My reward was to carry these bundles home. I wonder if any of you remember carrying home that warm package that once was a living chicken. It's a wonder I eat chicken today.

On occasion, Grandmother and I went to the local cinema, where they highlighted many Russian and other ethnic movies as well as American cinema. I would usually fall asleep. I do remember one specific time when the *Hunchback of Notre Dame* was playing. I was so frightened I had my head in her lap with my eyes closed. I recently saw the same movie this past year. Sir Charles Laughton was a magnificent actor to carry that part off, and Maureen O'Hara wasn't too bad to look at, if I may say so.

My father, an insurance man, worked very hard and was perhaps the most giving and caring person I have ever met. He was a great writer and a motivational speaker. His mentor was Norman Vincent Peale, most notably the authority on the power of positive thinking. He also was a member of the Masonic Order. I write more about my father in the next chapter.

My mother was multitalented, a homemaker, an artist, an actress, and in her own right, a writer and contributor to a book on our family origin—a memory of a small group of Jewish pioneers who left their homes in Europe and South Africa and, with a remarkable degree of courage and determination, founded the colony of Edenbridge in Northern Saskatchewan, Canada. The land of origin of her family was Lithuania. She also was the contributor to my many neuroses as the rest of the story depicts. As an example, she was in a play called *The Lost Soul*. There was this strange man on stage touching her and even kissing her. (This made me quite anxious and jealous, and I cried.) Many people thought my mom looked like Norma Shearer, a well-known actress at that time. I even got to see Paul Muni in our local playhouse before he became a famous Hollywood star.

In the early days of my life, unbeknownst to the infant me, my mother developed fainting spells, sadness, and an inability to bond with me in an essential act called breastfeeding or holding me to her chest. Many years later, this condition, which is very serious, has been labeled postpartum depression. Again my grandmother, the wondrous matriarch, came to the rescue. It is possible that my early excessive dietary intake fed by Grandma led to eczema and eventual asthma. This all resulted in a form of guilt anxiety, another one of my troublesome features. Was I at fault? Was it my doing? Was it that I was sickly with asthma? But Mom often told me that the pain of giving birth to me convinced her to never have another child. (She rubbed it in, and that stain persists to this day, as does my yearning for a sibling.) Eventually, Mom got well with old-fashioned doctoring (iodine drops), plenty of bedrest, and her resilient, strong nature. I'm not sure I recovered from her malady. My guilt continued to be an early anxiety. Was it that the pain I caused denied other children the chance to enter into the world? So I had several forms of angst. You betcha, as a famous politician would say.

Mother had a nighttime job at Sears Roebuck and would have to walk home each night. This is complex number two. I would nervously peer through a windowpane until she finally came home. Unfortunately, many who have suffered from separation anxiety know the intensity of this neurosis, and none was more intense than mine. My grandmother would pull me through each crisis until we were all safe and sound around the kitchen table.

My mother, in addition to contributing a chapter to a book reflecting on her family's saga and journey from the old country to South Africa and ultimately to the wilds of early Canada, always reminded me that in their journeys back and forth, my grandmother gave birth to her in New York City. She then had dual citizenship in Canada and the United States.

My aunts, those who lived with us until they married, worked in retail jobs of all sorts. They were once dubbed secretaries, but today, with political and social correctness, would be known as administrative assistants. Given a chance to do things differently, they could have had careers that were not readily open to them then.

Chapter 2

• •

Oh! My Papa

Oh, my Papa, to me he was so wonderful
Oh, my Papa, to me he was so good
No one could be so gentle and so lovable
Oh, my Papa, he always understood
—"Oh! My Pa-Pa"

"O mein Papa" is a German song and was adapted into English by John Turner and Geoffrey Parsons under the title "Oh! My Pa-Pa."

This song certainly fits my dad to a T. My father was special in so many respects. As the saying goes, he would give you the shirt off his back. My dad worked very late hours, and I would see him every night at 10:50 p.m. working on his debit books, as he called them. Although I did not see much of him otherwise and we never had heart-to-heart father-to-son talks, my love for him burned deeply in my heart.

He left a Ukrainian village at the age of three and settled in Omaha, Nebraska. At one point, he moved to California, made a fortune, and lost it overnight because the boss's daughter was involved. Without a nickel to his name, he called upon a dear friend to give him passage to Chicago. While in Chicago, he worked at many jobs, initially as a sheriff's bailiff, ultimately transitioning into the insurance business. My dad's family came from a small village called Linevski, and most of the family became Lehnofsky or Lehnoff in this country. When my grandfather Joseph came to this country with his poor English, the immigration officer at Ellis Island, pulling a name out of the air, named him Levin. This is reminiscent of an old Jewish joke: When an immigrant was asked his name, he replied in Yiddish German, "Ich hab schoen vergessen" (I have forgotten), so he was cleverly named Sean Ferguson.

My dad's nature may have been tempered by the toils and troubles of his early life. Both of his parents died at the early age of forty-five, his mother from a toxic goiter and his father, an inner ear infection that led to meningitis. He also had a brother, Samuel, who was injured at birth by being dropped on his head. I remember visiting him in a home in Dunning, Illinois. Uncle Samuel was a wonderful musician and was able to pick up any song by ear. I wonder if this may be the genetic connection to my musical talent.

My parents wed on a leap year. There is an article, which appeared in the Saturday edition of the *Herald American* 1932. Let me quote it verbatim. Mom states: "Here's how the leap year pressure is properly applied according to my mind. When those midnight whistles started blowing, I realized that opportunity was knocking. She who hesitates is lost. So I popped the question." My dad's answer: "I was caught in a weak moment. I blushed, murmured, 'This is so sudden,' and coyly rested my head on her shoulder." That, my friends, is typical of my dad's nature. They were married January 10, 1932.

My mom had been writing to my dad for months, and I recently read some of her steamy love letters to him.

"Love Letters"
Heyman/Young Composer
Sung by Elvis Presley
Love letters straight from your heart
keep us so near while apart
I'm not alone in the night
when I can have all the love you write.

It seems that in that gentler time of life (technology had not yet become so pervasive) letter-writing was common. One could not tweet, email, or fax. There was no Facebook or passive communication. It was in-your-face direct communication, and it was common where distance separated two people, such as my mom and dad in their courtship days. As we refer to it today, it was regular posting by snail mail or, if you had one, a standard telephone.

At this point, my father was spending time on an uncle's farm in New Jersey. He probably had some life crisis or depression based on his loss of a fortune in California. It was not his fault but that of a partner who cheated him.

The following is from a letter written by my mother to her love, my dad, dated August 14, 1931:

Received all your letters this morning, for which I thank you.
It sure made me feel much better since I received the picture
of my handsome Adonis. The cards are so cute and only you
would think of sending such adorable sayings to me.

Don't worry about me cheating. I told you in front of mother last Saturday night that I won't exchange you for all the money and riches in the world and that is a broad statement to make. I mean, it's from the bottom of my heart; the boys here are real nice but none as nice as you. You know your own song "in my eyes."

Another letter from my mom, dated June 16, 1931, reads:

Dearest Marty:

Although I have been warned against writing to members of the male sex, the temptation is so strong that I cannot resist. I am therefore taking this dangerous step by writing to an experienced correspondent, who no doubt has taken many such chances himself. Truthfully, I haven't had many dealings with men through correspondence (nor in any other way) that is not saying that I ever intended to.

Where formerly I would have had to be subpoenaed to enter into a written document, especially with one of the opposite sex; now, seemingly, it is second nature to me since meeting up with the aforesaid party of the second part. Then my vocabulary was a hidden virtue and words failed me. But since then thought and ideas, with unceasing regularity, flow like the proverbial stream.

I can see a lot of nice things. If as in my dreams, a certain party were in close proximity, the moon was suspended in its entire splendor on the new heavens above and shining down lighting the way to thrilling romance. But wait a moment. I'm getting ahead of myself and can't be held responsible for everything I said.

Well, being an amateur in the art of letter writing. I believe I made enough commitments for one of my tender age and so I will take my pen out of hand to continue when the second installment shall have been written by the party of the second part.

Wow! I had no idea that this was such a steamy romance and that my mother not only did write in a teasing manner but that she was out to capture her mate. I thank you, Mom, for your persistence, your humor, and your outright campaign to capture your mate.

There is a similarity here because I too was not very aggressive and needed a nudge to follow my dreams. I knew that my dad was very handsome from pictures I've seen. Women are persistent. History repeated itself in my courtship of Donna (or vice versa), albeit we went around it in a different manner. We did not write to each other; we used the telephone a lot, met somewhere for a soda or ice cream, and visited each other at our homes. In some manner, we communicated with our hearts. It was a mutual knowing that we were meant to be. And much like my mother did to my dad years earlier, my wife proposed to me.

My father would do anything for me and spent a lifetime going out of his way driving me to Navy Pier, the branch extension of the University of Illinois, where I went to premed, even though he worked in the Western suburbs. He always said it was on his way. It was not on his way, but it was his way to have some alone time with me, and I enjoyed it! That's another example of my pop's nature through and through. He would constantly do things for others willingly. When

Donna and I were married and I was a busy doctor, my dad would frequently visit our home and volunteer to do her shopping, bring in our laundry, and putter around in our garden.

I will now celebrate my dad through his own personal writings and tributes from a loving family.

My dad I were two peas in a pod. Incidentally, Donna, many years later, proposed to me as did my mother to my dad. Who says women's lib hasn't been around forever? As for what others in my family thought of Dad, here's a testimonial from my youngest aunt: "In as much as I am the youngest of the Louis and Rachel children, I deem it a great honor to toast you both on this joyous occasion. To Sara, our beloved sister, we bless and thank you for all the good deeds you have done for us. From the moment we were born. And whenever we needed you … And to you, dear Martin, our brother-in-law, but who has proven to be a true and real brother, full of love and devotion and always by our side."

That was a great way to describe my father. I found this prayer in his old writings, called "My Daily Prayer."

> If I have caused a tear to fall, in thought or words or deed,
> please God, I beg you to forgive—your help, I greatly need.
>
> If I have led one soul astray or fostered doubt and fear—
> erase the evil from my heart.
> Oh God, please linger near—Grant me faith to understand
> what happens in this life and strength so I can carry on.
> When caught in webs of strife, replace my hate with
> sincere love.
> Love is the magic cure needed by all mankind to make
> this long endure.

Let me do something good each day, however great or small.
Watch over my family and friends, and those who planned my fall.
My God reach out involve my heart when life is hard to bear.
Forgive me when I turned from you—this is my daily prayer.

You can see in this writing that Dad, in his earlier life, suffered much as one can read into his solution to avoid unnecessary hatred and replace it with a form of unconditional love. Incidentally, my dad was a songwriter. This became a source of one of his regrets, as he trusted the recording studios. Some of his songs were actually recorded without any credit given to him.

My children are a testimony to this, through the love they had for their grandfather, whom they called Zadie Marty (*zadie* being an old Yiddish term for grandfather, also *zayde*). A grandmother was called *bubbe* or *bubby*. It has a Slavic heritage, as one thinks of the women in Russia known as the *babushkas*.

Now let me quote a bit of his personal philosophy, which my mom and then I preserved to this very day. It was in a journal filled with his writings.

Freedom of choice: man is free to choose between good and evil. Accordingly, he is responsible for his actions. Therefore, he is eligible for a reward, and also deserving of punishment for what he does. The choice is his.
This life of ours is full of ups and downs with that you will agree.
We never know from day to day.
What things will come to be?

Sometimes we're in, often times we're out. It's funny but it's true.

We hardly know the joy of life before it says that adieu.

It seems that in our quest for gain. We never quite succeed.

For after we have reached our goal, we have a further need.

So on and on without a stop and 'round and 'round we go.

Hardly ever satisfied with the happiness we know.

And when the final curtain falls, our hearts are just content.

We realize the mistakes we made throughout the years we spent.

But there is no need to go astray as on through life, we plod.

For we can gain true peace of soul by living close to God.

Other thoughts from Dad:

- Watch your tongue; it is bound to be slippery, for it is always wet.

- Every person is composed of three characters: the one he is, the one he thinks he is, and the one he should be.

- Sometimes one might search the world over for something one thought one had missed, overlooking it right in front of one's eyes.

- The thing that goes the furthest toward making life worthwhile, that costs the least and does the most, is just a pleasant smile.

I once saw this saying on this wonderful grandfather's birthday card from his three grandchildren. Times have changed. Grandfather no longer sits in the rocking chair vegetating, nor does he wear long, white whiskers. He didn't feel any older with each grandchild and said they added years to his life. He was interested in many sidelines, such as doing things with his grandchildren and helping Mom care for them, and was quickly mobile and always coming to his grandchildren's events. They say it is wonderful to be a father—indeed, but one has to be one before he can work his way up to the role of grandfather.

My parents were always very active in helping others. I had prepared something for an event where my parents were being honored for years of service to the community. I called it "The Measure of Life."

The Measure of Life

Seconds fly, minutes fly, the days and weeks assemble.
Before the awesome end of time, a humble man must tremble.

By what measure can one determine our worth.
Can numbers alone speak for good deeds on earth?
Is it how much we have, how little we give.
How numerous our possessions or how long we live.

I see numbers are worthless in description of man.
There are measures far greater,
I'll explain if I can.
As a product of two, as a father of three, as a husband to one,
That's what life's worth means for me.

Seconds fly, minutes fly, the days and weeks assemble.
Before the awesome hand of time, a humble man must tremble.

Once in this large city, in the days before my birth.
Two people united for their lifetime on earth.
With days bringing hardships, they strived along the way.
To lead a life of purpose, to signify each day.

Working, striving, tirelessly paving a single road
Sharing all fortunes and sharing each load.
Mind and bodies joined together,
Each minute, each hour all kinds of weather

They performed the missions of their Lord
Doing for others was their reward.
Before time they did not cower.
Because, their love gave them power.

Seconds fly, minutes fly, the days and weeks assemble.
Before the awesome end of time, a humble man must
tremble.

My father worked a tedious day with purpose and resolve.
My mother working by his side, the family did evolve.
Just one child, nurtured by love, all early trials endured.
They worked so hard on their difficult path.
So my future would be assured.

Time meant many things to them ticking to their fate
Intimate time to love, to cry, to listen and create.
Good times, joyous times, help others every way.
And always time for their little son to wipe a tear away.

Seconds fly, minutes fly the days and weeks assemble.
Before the awesome end of time, a humble man must tremble.

The grade is measured, in endless ways,
what my parents gave to me.
A gift that cannot end with time,
it lasts eternally.

'Tis love you gave, this precious gift.
I can't assume its measure.
No day or hour can spend its worth
For it's everlasting treasure.

One can love in portion or degree,
Theirs a constant notion
Right now I feel so deep within
The everlasting devotion.

Seconds fly, minutes fly, the days and weeks assemble.
Before the awesome end of time, I fear I sometimes tremble.

But joy today, gladness, for all
You've succeeded all the way.
From a loving son I repeat
You are as yesterday

Tho silver crowns have come at last
The golden years can't age thee
From childhood to now, and all days past.
You are the same to me.

Your special love has multiplied
From your hearts to my own
In fullest measure in endless degree,
This love is grown and grown.

The seconds have flown, minutes have flown, days and years go by
Before the awesome hand of God, I'll love you till I die.

And it was indeed passed on to my wife, multiplied by my children, and never divided or taken away. If this love could fill the world, there'd be peace on earth each day. So, dear parents, let us not fear time, live each day as before, and when God gives you ten more years together, I'll beg him for ten years more!

As you can see from the poem above, both the Vickar and Levin part of me are literate, but I was done in by the quite strong Vickar emotion and Levin sincerity. Within minutes or seconds of starting to read this poem, I started to choke up and my dear aunt Ada had to read the poem for me.

My father was a loving, kind, gentle man. He passed away on April 2, 1975. Then there was my mother, who was so talented in many ways, as well as a beautiful woman early in life and elegant always. She then died September 21, 1995. They who gave birth to me, nurtured me, sacrificed for me, sustained me, and counseled me will always remain a part of me. They made me what I am to this moment. To this very day, they are missed but never forgotten.

Chapter 3

. . . .

Donna's Origins

I wish that I knew more about Donna's origins. Her last name implies she is most probably of Polish descent. All of the older generations in her family have succumbed to a genetic predisposition to cancer, and the knowledge has been lost. No one took the time to put it into writing. Donna was frustrated over this, and Ancestry.com was not on the scene for many years. We once traveled to Salt Lake City to search through the vast Mormon catacombs and databases. No luck there!

Donna's mother was of English origin (family name Edwards), and the family came from Manchester. I thank my mother-in-law, Rachel, of blessed memory, for delivering the love of my life.

There are some things that I know anecdotally. Donna had two younger siblings, Larry and Michael, whose memory of those times can't be recorded, as they have not been in contact with me since Donna's death.

I know that her dad was a physician in the US Army during World War II. He was initially assigned to the invasion of Italy but fell ill during that campaign. He was sent home in charge of German prisoners of war who were sent to various internment camps in this country. The prisoners of war were so grateful to this kindly physician that they never missed the opportunity to give him freshly baked bread, no matter what camp he was assigned to. I'm quite sure that many of these prisoners ultimately became US citizens.

Donna was an army brat, traveling from camp to camp with her folks and siblings. There is an interesting anecdote much repeated in the family. While her mom and dad were looking for a place to live, Donna was in charge of watching her younger brothers. When one of the brothers misbehaved, she vigorously pulled on his arm and dislocated his shoulder.

When the family finally arrived back in the city after her father's military service ended, they settled in a small apartment before buying a home on Lunt Avenue in East Rogers Park. It was at that time that President Gerald Ford's wife lived in the same area. There were also some very special talented people who were neighbors in Chicago and then moved to California where they became famous actors, producers, and directors. You remember Jerry Paris, the dentist neighbor in the *Dick Van Dyke Show*? He lived right across the street from her.

Donna's father became a well-known physician and one of the first who began his practice on the far north side of Chicago in an area called Rogers Park. It seemed that everyone knew him wherever he went. I remember his shingle hanging over a drugstore on Morse Avenue in Chicago.

I also heard from Donna that somewhere in her early years, she contracted polio and was paralyzed in one limb. Through the grace of God or luck, this did not progress to bulbar polio and on to a very serious condition. However, years later, her specialized doctors felt that she had post-polio syndrome, which added to the overall joint condition.

Years later, when Donna's cousin Stu put a video together reflecting on their youthful times as a family, I was able to see glimpses of my wife-to-be as a young child, ever smiling, as her family enjoyed times together. There is not a picture in my home in which Donna does not have that beautiful smile.

To learn more about Donna, I asked her best friend for the longest time, Diana, about her. She remembered the house was considered large (to those who lived in apartments) and that it was a friendly, warm home. She told me that one of her earliest memories of being with Donna was when television first came out. Donna's family had the earliest TV set that her friend could remember, and on Tuesday nights, when Milton Berle was on, Donna's family had people over to see the show. They set up chairs in the dining room, theater style, and loved being together.

Donna and her friend also baked a lot of goodies there (no wonder they both turned out to love baking so much). Donna's friend remembered going downtown on occasion to the Chicago Theater for a movie and live stage show, seeing Frank Sinatra and many other celebrities. They would go to the alley near the stages afterward to get some autographs. They would then go to the nearby Walgreens and have ice cream sundaes on a Saturday evening. They always traveled by subway. (This is a personal comment; I feel the subway was a lot safer in those days.)

When they got to high school, Donna joined a sorority, and as a group, they would go to the downtown Marshall Field's store and look at cashmere sweaters. I still have a box from one of them, even though the sweaters are long gone. I am sure that Donna saved her sweater, as she had to pay for it, working at Mandel Brothers Department Store.

Diane told me a few of her memories of their younger days.

"The summer we graduated Sullivan High School, we went on a trip to the West Coast and Catalina Island. This was our first airplane ride and our first earthquake experience. It was quite frightening.

"We slept over at Donna's house many times, and little brother Mike would bother us, asking if we had an extra bedroom for my brother, but we did not. I don't remember Larry being around much. Because they had what was considered a large home (compared to us who lived in apartments), we usually slept over there. It was a friendly, warm home. Once I remember the girls wanted to experiment with bleaching hair. Another girl Lois was with us that night, and my hair was the only one that we did not like at all. Since we were all shy, a group of us formed our own group titled the TASC, which meant the Tuesday after School Club."

The rest of the Diane's story occurs after I met Donna, and that is another time. You see, over time, Diane and her husband, Don, and Donna and I became very close friends.

I received another letter from Donna's friend Joyce. Joyce said she had very little independence as a child. "And so, my interaction with the group was very limited. My mother was overprotective." (Tell me about it, Joyce.)

Joyce states that she received a two-wheeled bike for her eleventh birthday, and that summer, Diane, Donna, Lois, and she biked to a park called Indian Boundary. This was west of us in West Rogers Park. However, since Joyce had to ride on the sidewalk, everyone was far ahead of her most of the time.

Donna was not into swimming and sunbathing, and Joyce spent most of the summers at the beach. (It may be because of this that Donna had beautiful skin and a beautiful complexion most of her life.)

Donna and Joyce would have more interaction later. They would gather on her front porch and listen to all the records Donna got from her uncle Harold. Joyce always enjoyed those times and considered them quite a treat. For the most part, Joyce remembers listening to only classical music at home.

Joyce stayed at Donna's house when her folks went to Florida on vacation. Believe it or not, this was after our first year of college, but Joyce had to stay there because her parents wouldn't leave her alone. "I had a wonderful time, and we enjoyed each other's company," Joyce told me. "I was actually allowed to do that on several occasions."

Joyce also remembers bridal showers, telling me, "Donna and her mom hosted bridal showers at their home for each of us, and we always felt welcome there. We were like one big happy family with all the parents liking each other."

This description of Donna easily embellishes my image of a loving friend whose home was open to all. She was kind, though a bit shy, and felt comfortable with a small group of friends. I do know that she had a boyfriend who admired her, and they often went to school together until his mom sent him to a private school. Many years later, Donna shared a letter from him where he reflected on his earlier good old days and how she was very special to him in many ways. He was living in New Mexico and was married by then. This was just a nostalgic note from him. That would be the kind of girl I would've liked to have known. Thankfully, I captured her for myself.

Chapter 4

• •

My Roots

"O Canada" (Richardson Version)
O Canada! Our fathers' land of old
Thy brow is crown'd with leaves of red and gold.
Beneath the shade of the Holy Cross
Thy children own their birth ...

My mother knew this song as well as the national anthem "God Save Our Gracious Queen," and I heard her sing this many times, as that was where she lived until she was sixteen years old and then came to Chicago. This, of course, made me curious about my own heritage. How or why did she get to leave home and land up in Chicago. The story is that she wanted to be a nurse, but for some reason, my grandfather did not like that idea, so he sent her to be the au pair for some Chicago relatives, who operated a small hotel and needed someone to look after their girls.

My maternal grandparents, along with their children and a band of Lithuanians, of late from South Africa, came to Canada, entering through Halifax Bay in Nova Scotia. My grandfather, along with two brothers and three sisters, ultimately emigrated to Saskatchewan, Canada, with the intent of forming a farming community. The youngest sister, a survivor of the Holocaust, was brought to Canada by her siblings.

My grandparents had one son and seven sisters, one who lost her life on the long voyage across the seas and is today buried in an unknown grave in Winnipeg, Canada. It is important to remember that my mom was born in New York City. This becomes essential to the story.

The role of the woman who arrived in Canada some hundred years ago was that of wife, mother, and worker. She rarely worked outside the home because she cleared homesteads, worked in the fields, tended the garden, watered and fed the cattle, reared children, and participated in some aspects of community life. Uncle Charles was born in South Africa, as was the next oldest child, the daughter who died after contracting some infectious disease while at sea. My mother, in a fortuitous circumstance, was a New Yorker and the rest of the children Canadian born.

There was a disadvantage at play here; Grandfather had one son and six daughters. His brothers had a flock of boys and an occasional daughter. Guess who was successful in the farming business. The brothers flourished as farmers, whereas my grandfather did not. He became the local justice of the peace and the authority in settling quarrels between the various ethnic groups that formed their own communities close together. He remained a scholar, a legislator, and a writer but never was a farmer.

My grandmother was called the Angel at the Side of the Road, as she was the daughter of a European doctor with knowledge of healing herbs and vegetation. In the absence of modern medication, she was able to help many people with her knowledge.

They managed to survive the wilderness for a while until Grandmother had enough. She was grieving the loss of her eldest child. They left the farm for relatives in New York, engaging my brilliant grandfather in the making of window shades or some other sundry activity. This venture did not last very long, and soon, they were back in the old shack. When they returned, the rest of the family was on their way to becoming successful farmers. They were entrepreneurs, opening a country store and starting to repair farm equipment or purchase new farm equipment for others. Years later, this evolved into their becoming successful owners of car dealerships. My grandfather's sisters also gave up their farm life and moved to Winnipeg. The youngest sister, who may have been affected by the war in Europe, was cared for by the brothers and eventually married.

Grandmother, while still on the farm, got along with the many Ukrainian immigrants and the aboriginal Americans living in her community. As in many large families, she allowed the eldest daughter to care for her growing group of children. She was the prize of the neighborhood, having trained with her father, Dr. Gordon. She knew the value and danger of many herbs and plants growing in the wild fields of early Canada.

Growing up, I spent Summers in Canada to avoid the Chicago heat, ragweed, and mold that led to my frequent asthmatic attacks. We would spend many summers up north in Edenbridge, Saskatchewan, and little towns like Brooksby, Star City, and Melfort. These times were my chance to see my Canadian relatives and visit where my mother grew up. This was my main summertime event: a return to my mother's homestead and village in Canada.

We usually drove to Canada. I would keep busy singing folk songs while my father was busy smoking away with his nickel cigars. The windows were all closed. We begged him to stop, but it was many years later before he did so. I certainly was exposed to a lot of secondhand smoke in a household of cigarettes and Dad's cigars. Incidentally, my mother and Aunt Betty succumbed to lung cancer, as did a younger cousin. One dear cousin, Carol, who has had her share of medical issues has now developed lung cancer. When you are young, you do not think of illness. Today, it weighs heavily on a broken heart.

There are many things that stand out for me, the young city boy down on the farm. Most of them were fun for me but annoying for my relatives. Many tractors and farm implements were laid waste by those precious fingers. I constantly allude to my mother's protectiveness of my fingers lest my musical career end abruptly.

The farm animals were not all friendly to me. Yes, I learned to milk the cows, attempted to ride horses, and avoided the ever-present chickens and the strutting roosters. My chief nemesis was one goose that kept chasing me all over the farm. This again elicited the famous maternal family cry and a lot of laughs from my relatives.

One of the nicest things I remember about the farm was a summer kitchen, where there was always fresh milk (unpasteurized, I'm sure), fresh recently churned butter, and that warm homemade bread. This country living was a great way to bed down early and to rise with expectation and wonder as to what would come next on the following day.

I do remember driving a car freely down the dusty backgrounds with no one to ticket me. There was no one to test me or arrest me, and I hate to tell my family that I had no driver's education. Back in the city, my dad would let me drive in some empty lot. I always wondered why he had his hand on the door as if he wanted to escape.

Another form of driving was driving huge nails into the back of a great uncle's pickup truck. Of course, he was angry, but he dared not start any conflicts with my mother, my great defender. By that time, I had already been nicknamed Dennis the Menace. My mother always protected me by warnings to others that any provocation or undue excitement could precipitate an asthmatic attack. I'm beginning to think that my mother fought my battles for me (and was a great con artist at it, don't you think?).

Anyhow, several days later while riding the same truck, I was given a reprieve. Bad move! I let uncle's prize pig out of the truck, and there was a great deal of tumult running down the road trying to capture it. This time, his anger was visceral, and there was a lot of muttering under his breath. We quickly left that relative to visit others who had moved to bigger cities like Winnipeg, Melfort, Saskatoon, and even that great city in the east, Toronto. As the saying goes, what a relief it was to enjoy indoor plumbing and escape the outhouse back on the farm. It must've been a relief for those kindly folks who endured all the mischief I presented them with.

Returning to the farm and the country store run by Grand-Uncle David, I ran into many Socialists and anarchists who had left Europe (and often their families behind), but their views prevailed, especially their dislike of the United States. In my own manner, I remember defending my country vigorously and as best as I could. I even resorted to tears, as I could not hold them back.

There was an older cousin, Edward, who called my dad a very strange name, Poopadack Pappy. I had no idea where the term came from, but his tease always got to me, and I perpetually reverted to the cry. I have done a little research on this family cry. Experts say that there are a number of factors or scenarios that cause crying. It is commonly caused by depression, stress, or pain. Crying is a natural way our bodies releases stress or pain. It is helpful in the natural functioning of the body. Crying could be caused by a number of situations and factors. Sometimes you don't know why you're crying at all, but the human body knows when it needs an emotional release. The limbic system and parasympathetic branch of the autonomic system control glands and production of emotions and reactions. When receptors are activated because of emotional feelings, a gland called the lacrimal gland produces our tears. (Please excuse me; that's the physician in me.)

Mind you, this cry of mine comes on at a moment's notice, be it a happy, emotional, or sad event, and I have witnessed this in many of my relatives. Seemingly, it is not always at holiday times or when someone has passed away but also at joyous occasions where emotion gets to me.

I can't imagine that my maternal ancestors all suffered from some serious illness incurred from an infected mad cow or that some crazy angry goose in a little village in Europe led our family to crying from generation to generation with or without reason. We are just an emotional family and should accept it, try to control it, and not seek answers. A little later on, I will give you an example of my crying for joy ...

On the day I was going home, I carried a baby chick home with me as a pet. I gave it my best shot trying to conceal it, but alas, it was discovered and quickly removed from my pocket and turned over to the authorities. Need I say this? Out came my inherited and by then famous ready cry. I was quickly shuffled onto the train and promised a trip to the dining car. Not only an army travels well on its stomach, so did chubby Joel.

I guess you can say our family is unbalanced in some many ways. They call it dysfunctional today. I constantly hear this from the squabbling relatives. But is that not so of many families? We all have our quirks and our family jerks. Forgive me if I insult the perfect family somewhere out there.

I forgot to tell you that Canada is very much like the States, as the only restaurants along the lonesome road were Chinese. This seemed to be the special industry of the Chinese in early Canada, if not building the railroads. The food was not very special and not at all like Chinese American (US) food.

We returned to the farm many more summers until my teenage years and the improvement of my allergy had been established. In truth, by then, I was more interested in trying my luck with the ladies than traveling with my parents. Years later, with that land lying fallow and most of the Canadian relatives having moved to bigger cities, the farm was sold back to the government. Thus ends this section. There is still a lot more to tell, and faith has not delivered me to my beloved.

This ends the story of my family's arrival in Canada, their coming to the States, and then my wonderful and exciting opportunity to see where we came from. It allowed me to establish some maternal roots. I never had that opportunity with my dad's family. The gist of the story is that my mother, as an American citizen, was able to bring her whole family to the United States and specifically to the city where I was born.

I will always remember my times at the farm in Canada, and I still remember that walk-up apartment where we all lived in Chicago. It was warm, cozy, and my cocoon and escape from a confusing world. But as Tony Bennett sang, I was "without a song" to call my own as yet. Oh yes, each day, I would say, "Let my life begin." There was a yearning deep within me for something more that was yet to be.

Chapter 5

My Quiet Room and Quiet Life

I have a quiet room, a room nobody can see
A secret place that's all my own
And only I have the key
Where I live apart and alone
—"Quiet Room," words and music by Fred
Hellerman and Fran Minkoff, sung by Harry Belafonte

In this crowded house filled with love and a lot of excitement, I really
lacked for nothing in those days except at times a room of my own.

I did have a room of my own at some point. I wish to return to my
initial premise promising to make this a fun book as well as a serious
work for all to peruse and enjoy. Believe me if you will, it was in or out,
depending on who moved in or moved out of our house. For the most part,
I had to share a room, first with my parents and then aunts and cousins.

I lost my bedroom when an uncle died at an early age and two
cousins and my aunt came home to be with us. I gained surrogate

siblings but lost my beloved room. My new designated space was on a cot bed in a tiny sun parlor I shared with my older cousin Sam, who was more like a brother to me. Aunt Betty and Cousin Leila occupied my once-beloved bedroom.

Finally, as the crowd cleared out over the years, I had that bedroom back to myself. This was not to last. Some ladies of the night and of questionable virtue moved next door. I found it quite interesting watching them wave, shimmy, and seductively glance at the boys in the neighborhood. In truth, I peered through my window at night as any young man seeking further education and vicarious satisfaction would do. Once my parents caught on to this, we moved and my peeping Tom period came to an end. I may have been experiencing lust as some in higher stations of life have spoken of or acted upon.

As I was growing up in a household with people at various ages and stages of life, I had a little trick when my youngest aunt was not yet married and was still living at home. As a clever youth, I actually made a living by placing myself in the parlor while Aunt Marge and Uncle Leo (to be) were courting and spooning. (What an old-fashioned word!) My economic game seemed so legal. Maybe it was. My court(ing) fee cost the young suitor $.25 cents each time trying to get me to go play elsewhere. "Get lost, young fella!" (vamoose) is more precise.

When at last I had my own room, I would spend my evenings listening to the radio. Before the era of television, sitting around the radio was a popular form of home entertainment. Radio was not only a medium; it embellished my young emotions, provided entertainment and information, and served as a warning beacon during emergencies, such as it was during the Great War (World War II). Radio has been so important in our culture. We have sung songs about it and exclaimed how it's helped us, changed us, comforted us, and consoled us. It certainly did for me.

Radio then, not as today, starred many top-name radio and film stars. During the golden age of radio, networks also broadcast kids' adventure shows, thrillers, westerns, comedies, and quiz shows like Dr. I.Q. (I have a lady or gentleman in the balcony and a question was asked and followed by "give him/her ten silver dollars").

I enjoyed the radio show called *I Remember Mama*, which was initially a play by John Van Druten. Based on the fictionalized memoir *Mama's Bank Account* by Kathryn Forbes, it focused on the Hanson family, a loving family of Norwegian immigrants living at 115 Steiner Street (identified as Larkin Hill in the 1948 film) in San Francisco in the 1910s, and I believe it was the Lux Radio Hour. Recently, I watched the movie once again on the Turner Classic Movie channel.

Since I have more than a pinch of nostalgia within me, I know it as "old-time radio" and thoroughly enjoy these nostalgic recordings today, especially the mystery programs. It is no wonder that in this day and age, I listen to old radio classics and watch ME TV (Memorable Entertainment Television, the oldies and goodies of television) and the Turner Classic Movie channel. I enjoyed *The Lone Ranger, Tom Mix*, and *Jack Armstrong, the All-American Boy*. For young readers, there were even interactive programs. A very professionally created two-man operation, *Calling All Detectives*, had a quiz show element to its detective format. This was my favorite and a frustration for me. A Mr. Paul Barnes, master of many voices, played all the characters. The only other man on the set was the sound-effect man. Barnes played Detective Browning. The show was a short drama, followed by a commercial break while Paul Barnes dialed a number often to people who never listened to the program.

Didn't he know that the master detective, yours truly, was ready to be his Kojak, Sam Spade, Johnny Dollar, etc.? Alas, I was a "shadow" to him. The idea was that a telephone number from the phone book was randomly called while the listener tried to figure out the answer to the mystery. The clue was usually an address, a telephone number, a name of the villain, or a car license. Paul then came back on the radio to finish the drama. I was always ready with pencil and notepad, looking for clues, as I felt him speaking directly to me.

Random calls did not quite work, as many who received calls never were as avid as I was, so later Barnes decided it would be better to call only those who were listening to the program. Listeners sent in cards in hopes that their name would be drawn that week and they would be able to solve that week's mystery on the air. Unfortunately, I, lying in bed with my Dick Tracy watch, decoder ring, and detective pad and pencil, fortified with my Ovaltine, was ever ready but never got the call. Perhaps it was somebody on our two-party line (a shared line) gabbing away or claiming the prize of CDOWS (chief detective of the West Side). This show taught me perseverance, a lasting quality of mine. My dad was my role model with his "do it well or not at all" or "when the work is never done, see it through from dusk to dawn."

I enjoyed the big-band era—Tommy Dorsey, Jimmy Dorsey, Glen Miller, Count Basie, Dizzy Gillespie, Louie Armstrong, and Benny Goodman. This was the era of jazz, and Louie Armstrong stands out in my mind. How many remember Spike Jones and his City Slickers? Spike Jones (1911–1965) was an American musician and bandleader specializing in performing satirical arrangements of popular songs. The Jones treatment would be punctuated with gunshots, whistles, cowbells, and outlandish vocals. "Cocktails for Two" was one of my favorites. Do you remember the comedic rendition?

In some secluded rendezvous,

that overlooks the avenue,

with someone sharing a delightful chat,

of this and that, and cocktails for two.

I would laugh until that wheeze of mine came on. I was very asthmatic during my early years. Not being able to catch your breath is an awful experience, and there were no modern medicines in those days. My reward was that my dad always brought home some comic books for me. I should have saved them, as they would be collector items today.

Talking about my asthma and my sick days at home, I especially loved *The Kate Smith Hour* and waited for that glorious moment when she belted out "God Bless America." Kathryn Elizabeth Smith, known professionally as Kate Smith and the First Lady of Radio, was an American singer, an alto, best known for her rendition of Irving Berlin's "God Bless America." Smith had a radio, television, and recording career spanning five decades, which reached its pinnacle in the 1940s. She became known as the Songbird of the South after her enduring popularity during World War II and contribution to American culture. When she said, "Save your tinfoil and rubber bands," I joined her army of patriots.

To this day, I find a way to listen to old-time radio and watch the old classic movies.

There was an added advantage to living where we did. There was a roof garden at the old Jewish People's Institute (JPI) across the street on Douglas Boulevard. Every Sunday, they would have a band performing, and I can imagine all those young people swinging and swaying to the tunes. It was great added entertainment for me while lying in my bed just listening and enjoying the rhythms of a dance orchestra. As a young budding musician, this was a treat. Incidentally, there is a photograph in a local restaurant of the old west side of Chicago and that same roof garden. I was looking at it one day, when there before my eyes was a photograph of a young group in which, front and center, was my aunt Marge, who was a young teenager at the time. Today, she is ninety-three years old.

I also took my first piano lessons at the same institute. My first teacher was a Miss Rose Jaffe, who after a bit of time shot me up the ladder to more advanced teachers and the advancement of my musical career.

I remember once walking home at night from an after-school program and seeing a falling star. It was April 12, 1945, the birthday that Donna and I shared. I was eleven years old, and I had one of my recurring premonitions that something was wrong. Surely enough, when I got home, I found out President Franklin Delano Roosevelt had died that day. My family was crying.

As a youngster, I loved to read books, and there is a book that I still remember with fondness.

My favorite book, *A Tree Grows in Brooklyn*, kind of separated me from the "real boys" in my hood who preferred short reading material or books about cowboys and the old West. *A Tree Grows in Brooklyn* is a 1943 novel written by Betty Smith. The story focuses on an impoverished but aspirational third-generation-American adolescent girl and her ethnically blended family in Williamsburg, Brooklyn, New York City, during the first two decades of the twentieth century. The book was an immense success, and I still have my copy, which I can't give up. The Nolans lived in the Williamsburg slums of Brooklyn from 1902 until 1919. Their daughter Francie and their son Neely knew more than their fair share of the privations and sufferings that are the lot of a great city's poor. Primarily, this is Francie's book. She was an imaginative, alert, resourceful child. And Francie's growing up and beginnings of wisdom are the substance of *A Tree Grows in Brooklyn*. The main metaphor of the book is the hardy tree of heaven, native to China and Taiwan, now considered invasive and common in the vacant lots of New York City. Could this have been my metaphor to escape poverty, or did it play on my aspiration to become something else? That book still resonates with me today. I saw a lot myself in Francie.

Some might call this a literary imbalance with my school chums or just a proclivity to being odd. (I would be classified as a nerd in those days or some other special term used in my generation.) Who cares? We are all unique, I say.

I once read eighteen books during summer break from school. I played chess more than checkers, had a silkworm project, and had toy soldiers (until my mother learned that they were made out of lead!). I practiced the piano four hours per day. I also loved to write short stories, and for some reason, even then, my stories involved travels to other planets and beyond. Am I in some way related to a Jules Verne–type individual?

Living in Chicago, you were either a Chicago Cubs fan or a White Sox fan. Living on the West side of town, I could have gone either way. I chose the Cubs and for the most part would ride the elevated trains (the El) to Wrigley Field, usually with some cousins or with friends on occasion. We always sat in the bleachers, so I was a "bleacher bum." (*Bleacher Bums* was a 1977 play written collaboratively by members of Chicago's Organic Theater Company, from an idea by actor Joe Mantegna, a Cubs fan of renown.) I sat on the left field side and was quite a heckler in those days. The famous ivy-covered walls protected me, and I was fortunate enough never to be thrown out. There was nothing like Wrigley Field, the hot dogs, peanuts, soft drinks, and that wonderful feeling of the great outdoors. I remember Ernie Banks ("Let's play two"), Sweet Billy Williams, Ron Santo, Hank Sauer, and Hal Jeffcoat as some of my early favorite players. For some reason, I also remember the saying, "Smalley (shortstop) to Waitkus (first baseman) to grandstand." Roy Smalley had a very powerful arm, and at times, he contributed some great baseball souvenirs to the guys or gals sitting in the right grandstand. Oh yes, Waitkus was once shot by a fan (what a form of adoration), and our new first baseman was a kid called Chuck Conners. You would know him as the Rifleman. Today, after investing sixty or more years as a die-hard Cubs fan, I am a little more laid-back and never expect to see them in the World Series. Today, my allegiance is directed to our football team (Da Bears) and to the Chicago Bulls. I'll never forget watching Michael Jordan perform his magic and giving us repeat championships.

Another redeemer and balance to my life as a young boy, making me one with my friends was that I also loved to listen to the boxing matches fought by Rocky Marciano and Sugar Ray Robinson and the sheer glory and might of the "Brown Bomber," a boxer by the name of Joe Louis. He was my hero, a hero for all Americans. He was the defender of America when he pulverized Max Schmeling, who was Adolph Hitler's defender of the master race. My family was generally nonracist (as we were a minority), generally blind to a person's color or race, and never forgot that they themselves were recent immigrants. Yes, Joe was an American, and we loved Joe.

In these modern days, priests, reverends, rabbis, and pastors have made this into a religious or political agenda and formed well-meaning coalitions. The America that I grew up in was a rainbow coalition; a melting pot is what they called it. My school was multiethnic and multicultural with every race and creed represented. Yes, there were fights, turf wars, and fears of walking past the boundary of your neighborhood, as one ethnic neighborhood closely bordered another in our city. Black eyes and racial slurs were commonplace, and I experienced some of that. When I became a patrol boy in grade school because I stopped a kid from running across the street, I received some much-needed protection from a friend and the only boy with a mustache in grade school, Nick. One of the older brothers of this boy attacked me with a knife. (He was later imprisoned for multiple crimes.) What a neighborhood!

That generation remained very much ethnocentric and single-minded about their religious beliefs for some time. Even my grandfather did not let me go to the prom with a beautiful Italian girl, whom I adored. To be fair, he also said no to a family within our heritage who were dealing and wheeling to marry off their daughter. He was irate and gathered us all up to leave. I guess that was fair-minded, or he did not like this kind of trading of humans as merchandise. He always called me his professor. I was quiet and studious, and he felt that I was destined to be something special. He was a professional himself, a district judge in Canada and a journalist when he arrived in Chicago. I also think that he wanted me to have the chance to choose my own pathway in life. Thank you, Grandpa, for what was yet to be.

Going back to those times though, I think of that grand moment when turf wars were forgotten, when the Kellys and Cohens, the Mastersons and Maggios, all rose as one against a common enemy facing them during World War II. Many have called them the greatest generation.

Chapter 6

. . . .

My Yesterday

Yesterday, all my troubles seemed so far away
Now it looks as though they're here to stay
Oh, I believe in yesterday
—"Yesterday," the Beatles' Paul McCartney

For sure, I have a shadow hanging over me; I am only half of what I was in my earlier years. I long to return to the yesterday of my life but can only do it through this project.

During my early school days, I was a pretty good student and at an early age began my musical career. There was something within me that loved music, and from age four on, music, the piano especially, became a great part of my life. I started on a cardboard keyboard, advanced to a spinet, and ultimately moved to the love of my life, a Baldwin baby grand piano. Years later, with destiny playing its mystical hand, I looked inside at a bronze plaque in my piano. I saw that my buddy piano was born (manufactured, you sillies) the same year as I was.

I also had a grade-school vocal career. The funny part was that a certain teacher, Mrs. Grennan, made me part of the school Christmas pageant, with me having the highest voice in the caroling group. How embarrassing. It was with boys badgering (not actually bullying me) and girls twittering (not tweeting as one does today). But I never answered back, not being a Don Rickles (an American stand-up comedian widely known as an insult comic). I could never confront, be insulting, or push back. It took many holidays before my voice changed.

Music of course created a disadvantage, as I didn't get the chance to interact with boyfriends or play baseball or football for fear that I would hurt myself and those wondrous fingers that my mother always spoke about.

Here's another interesting tidbit from my early life. My older cousin and I were given roller skates. I think that I owned them for maybe an hour or so as my cousin in his eagerness put them on and immediately broke his leg in several places. There went my skates never to return. We also had a football for maybe an hour. I kicked it, and it went upward onto a roof. My mother thought I would try to retrieve it so that was the last of my young football career. I could never play football in the city lots or parks because of my musical career.

I also never owned a two-wheeler bicycle as it was too dangerous, as per my mother. It was years later when our children had bicycles that I taught them and then myself to ride a bicycle.

My earlier games were kick the can, red rover, and trying to master the yo-yo. There were marble games and hide-and-seek. I wonder if Mom knew that you needed a knife for some of the street games. We had less outdoor supervision in those days. We stayed outdoors until the sun went down or until Henry Aldrich was called home. Do any of you remember that name?

I do remember shopping with my grandmother and especially those wonderful moments as we walked home carrying a warm package, shall we say a recently deceased chicken or some creature of the sea, lake, or river. What a memory! The only fish I ever saw were packed on ice in the smelliest place on earth. There is this wonderful anecdote about chicken dinners, as most of the chickens we bought had unfertilized eggs in them. They were of different sizes, and of course the largest to the smallest were given by rank.

My grandmother actually was a great cook and breadmaker. Let the others be the breadwinners; a fair tradeoff, I would say—keep Grandma in the kitchen. I base this on my current love for the staff of life to this day. Let them eat cake, I would imperiously say. Actually, my mother was the champion of chocolate cake and my aunt Betty the doughnut queen.

Well-fed by all, I entered an amateur radio contest for young talents called *The Morris B. Sachs Hour*. I was asked by the host if I played football (of course not but guess why!). Little did he know about the house I lived in. My only sports activity was passing the bread around the table—a form of relay, I suppose? Let's just say I was a big boy who played the piano but did not participate in sports activities until years later.

I vaguely remember icehouses, coal shutes, and stables with horses in them. Corner groceries, not malls, and streetcars with tracks down many streets were part of my growing up. I remember World War I veterans who had lost their legs and ambulated on wooden platforms and those short of breath because of the gas used during the war. I remember men debating on many street corners, moms and kids sitting on stairways just relaxing and sleeping in the park on a hot summer night. That was our air conditioning, and one really needed to condition oneself to that humid air.

Look at what technology has wrought upon us or brought to us.

Thinking back to the simplicity of our language and how meanings change, let us humor ourselves with some of the radical changes.

There was no such thing as texting—but there were textbooks.

There was no iCloud—but the clouds in the sky there for your imagination.

There was no iPad—but working men needed to pad their knees and elbows for protection.

There was no TV for quite a while—the radio was dominant. To this day, I love my radio and connect to old-time programs that were once classic for me and today quite nostalgic.

There was no Google—but there was *Barney Google*, an American comic strip created by cartoonist Billy DeBeck. The initial appeal of the strip led to its adaptation to film, animation, popular song, and television. It added several terms and phrases to the English language and inspired the 1923 hit tune "Barney Google" (with the Goo-Goo-Googly Eyes).

Yahoo was not a website—but a yell of enthusiasm for a pleasurable moment or a success.

Chrome was not part of our personal computers—but real chrome was part of every car off of the assembly line.

Amazon.com did not exist—but the Amazon River and Amazon jungle were there.

There was no Nook reader (Barnes and Noble)—but a nook was a wonderful place to sit down and read a book. One summer, I actually read eighteen books from the day school was out to Labor Day.

Of course McDonald did not serve food—but as a farmer, he helped feed the nation.

And someone would say, "This is so fun," rather than "This is so much fun." Where have all the adverbs gone?

"Summertime" by George Gershwin

The few lines I know are:

> Oh, Your daddy's rich
> And your mamma's good-lookin'
> So hush, little baby
> Don't you cry …

Well, my daddy was never rich, my mama was certainly good-looking, and I was never in any cotton fields that George Gershwin spoke of but rather miles and miles of wheat fields during my trips to the province of Saskatchewan in Canada.

I participated in the styles and mannerisms of the times in the 1940s from zoot suits to baggy pants, marine-blue trousers with peg pants, army caps, and as long a keychain as one could find to wear. That was a bit of a disaster, as I always lost my keys, my glasses, or some article of clothing. That keychain cost my parents much more than it was worth considering all of the keys that needed to be replaced. I had, nevertheless, a need to have it all, very much trying to participate in the culture of that time. Kids were different in those days. A teenager's life in the 1940s, at least my life, was very different from those of today's kids.

There were no Levi's in my house but corduroys, no cell phones, but trying to understand cell structures at school. There were no flash mobs, but flashbulbs when using your camera. A summer job at the drugstore or ice-cream store was exciting, and being called a soda jerk was not offensive. But within this early stage of my life, television suddenly arrived with its small screens, the old rabbit-ear antennas, poor reception, and little programing. I would sit there and gaze at the television signal until a program came on. Wrestling was a biggy in those days, not as yet called WrestleMania. I will never forget my grandmother shouting, "Push him down!" and when there was boxing, my grandfather boxing right along, swearing in some mysterious combination of languages. For a very intelligent man, he could not understand the technology where people could appear on the screen. I remember (prior to his participation in boxing) his saying that there were ghosts or spirits entering our parlor through this strange new device.

Summertime also meant amusement parks. For the younger set, used to giant amusement parks, such as Five flags, Great America, and the Disney parks, Riverview Park was an amusement park in Chicago, Illinois, which operated from 1904 to 1967. It was located on seventy-four acres in an area bound on the South and East by Belmont and Western Avenues respectively, on the North by Lane Tech High School, and on the West by the North branch of the Chicago River. It was in the North Center community area and a neighborhood favorite family place on Chicago's north side.

Riverview was most known for the Bobs roller coaster. Other popular coasters were the Comet, the Silver Flash, the Fireball, and the Jetstream. Aladdin's Castle was a classic fun house with a collapsing stairway, mazes, and a turning barrel. Shoot the Chutes, Hades, the Rotor, Tilt-a-Whirl, Wild Mouse, the Tunnel of Love, and the Flying Cars were just a few of the many classic rides. "The Pair-O-Chutes at Riverview Park will shake us up all day" is a line from the Beach Boys' song "Amusement Parks USA" from their 1965 album Summer Days (And Summer Nights!!).

The Family

Sunday with my clan was kind of interesting, as this was the gathering of the family for a full day. All my cousins and their parents would come to our apartment, and there was a lot of bonding. Like all families, there were also many squabbles, which were quickly forgotten. The image I remember most was that of female dominance. Although my grandfather was the respected patriarch, we were a greatly matriarchal clan. My uncles and my dad were content to sit in the parlor, puff on their cigars, engage in small talk, and within minutes nod off. My grandfather retired to his den. I don't remember any organized activities among the kids, but we must all have been content playing indoors or outdoors together. A few times, we actually went to picnics in the forest preserves. My grandmother always brought her samovar. A samovar is a traditional device used to heat water for tea. The word *samovar* in Russian means "boils itself." Samovars can be found in homes throughout Russia and other Eastern European nations, as well as in Central Asia. I inherited the samovar, and it has the official seal "made in Russia." At these picnics, the young guys got their dads to join in the traditional baseball game.

Most of the kids had siblings except for me and another cousin, Susan, who was very quiet in those days, as I was. We had a quiet understanding (or resentment on my part) of being only children of our parents. The rest of the story regarding our relationship is yet to be told later on in this memoir. I was kind of jealous of being an only child, to tell the honest truth, with no brothers or sisters. This played into that nasty guilt complex and the now well-publicized fact that my mom hated childbirth (not me) and decided not to have any more children. She also suffered from that nasty postpartum depression, my fault of course, said I over and over again. I heard that I had caused her pain, and that was that. So I was content loving my cousins, mourning for denied siblings, and looking forward to Sunday with the clan.

The summary of my life to that time was music, school, family, and trips to the doctor.

Yes, yesterday was filled with confusion and the pangs of growing up, being not yet a man and not completely fulfilled as a growing boy. As the saying goes, neither saint nor sinner was I. I thus end this early chapter of my life from music to maladies to maidens of the night and move on to the rest of life. However, our beguine had not yet begun.

Chapter 7

• •

The Music Man

"Paper Doll" was written by Johnny Black (1915). My favorite version was the Mills Brothers'. It went something like this:

> I'm gonna buy a paper doll that I can call my own
> A doll that other fellas cannot steal

It ended with:

> I'd rather have a paper doll to call my own
> Then have a fickle real live girl.

A personal fugue:

> Bashful, bashful, I'm so bashful
> haven't got a clue as what to do
> Hormones flowing, feelings stirring
> My body seems to have the flu
> With gals around, I lose my tongue
> And out the window courage too.

I think actually my shyness got worse. Such were those next days of my life. I don't know if being an only son, feeling too comfortable or cloistered in my home life, or just a fear of trying new things led me to isolation and the pangs of growing up. By this, I mean going out with girls was so clumsy. Mind you, I was attracted to the opposite sex, but there is a great difference between having attraction and being successful at it. Today, they say it's all in the DNA and genetic makeup. To me, DNA in those days meant "do not attempt." I was afraid and much too shy to approach a girl in a one-on-one situation. In those days, they said it was just my nature and I was a very studious and quiet boy.

I was very clumsy at dating and at an earlier age could not put two words together when speaking with a girl. Ah, but I loved those old kissing games.

Let me give you some examples. These are some of the fiascoes I can recall while others remain repressed or simply forgotten.

My older cousin and I, for example, liked double dating—and we had this particular opportunity dating two daughters of a physician. All spruced up, I walked into the foyer and immediately knocked over a statue. That was the end of that evening.

The second encounter was going dancing with the neighborhood girl I was attracted to (or was I attracted to her father's restaurant?). On the way to the dance hall, I lost my glasses and was literally blind the rest of the evening. My new girlfriend (along with the advantage of free food at her father's delicatessen) quickly vanished from my life.

Sometime later while belonging to an organization called AZA, I agreed to date a girl from the female part of the organization (BBYO, Bnai Brith Youth Organization). For some reason, maybe like the character Wally from *Leave It to Beaver*, I (my parents) had invested (that is my parents invested) in a lovely corsage. During the evening, she lost my floral present, an orchid, for her. Anger got the best of me, and I refused to talk to her for the rest of the evening. She was a beautiful girl, but it was not to be.

Another date and another woe occurred when Mom fixed me up with the daughter of her boss. We went to the forest preserves with a group of guys and gals. At that stage of my life, I had a solid constitution, if you know what I mean. For some odd reason, on that fateful day, being very nervous for a change, that solid constitution fell apart and I resigned myself to constant visits to the old wooden privy and occasional visits to the girl. That was the end of that.

Probably the best evidence of a fumbling youth comes from when my friends decided to have a beach party. Naturally being quite naive, I had no idea of their plans. My plan was to be the entertainment of the evening, as that was what I was conditioned to do and that was all I knew. Being quite skillful with several musical instruments and quite unaware of the evening's true agenda, I brought my ukulele along. My friends had other intentions and were not planning on sitting around the fire singing folk songs.

"Good Night, Irene," lyrics by Steve Earle

Sometimes I live in the country
Sometimes I live in town
Sometimes I have a great notion
to jump into the river and drown.

Well, it wasn't a river but the Rainbow Beach. I had no intention of drowning except in my own misery.

In summary, it was my piano and me, my guitar and me, my ukulele or harmonica and me, almost anything that made music. Others had girlfriends, I had things that strummed, made chords, or made sounds but never made out.

I must add that Donna was not much of a dater either. She was content to be with her girlfriends and had one boy who lived on her block and liked to talk with her and walk her home. From her sources available to me (her girlfriends), she did not date. I wonder if she played post office as many of us did.

The Music Man

"Music Music Music" was a popular song written by Stephen Weiss and Bernie Baum and published in 1949. My favorite rendition was that of Theresa Brewer.

> So, put another nickel in
> in the nickelodeon
> All I want is lovin' you
> and music, music, music …

I wasn't a nickelodeon exactly, and it didn't cost a penny to hear me play. But I was on automatic during this period of my life whenever called upon to perform. And they may have loved my music, but I did not think they were loving me. They admired my playing, but the girls wanted a more traditional relationship. My piano would be in the way of alternative activities.

This herky-jerky period of my life and my inability to deal with the young foxy ladies (I would label this the fox-trot period of life) is what led me to the next phase of my life. I traded ten warm fingers for a gal for eighty-eight piano keys. My musical career continued on for years and perhaps was the only real self-gratification, or was it? My proud mother with her eagle eye discovered a piano, and it was, "Joel, play something for us." I will not dwell on this, but at one point, I went from Easter celebrations, Christmas pageants, and school performances to my music school recitals (where as top bill, I allowed my hands to get real cold and my anxiety to reach a pitch (all puns intended). There were fancy ladies' soirees on the Gold Coast and many a men's club organization.

I actually performed for the prisoners in a county jail. How frightening and how silent were the men in prison wearing their orange garb, and there was I with a greenish complexion … Mozart, Bach, Chopin, Beethoven, for these inmates, I think not. I am sure they envisioned other forms of entertainment. If only I was Johnny Cash.

> "Folsom Prison Blues"
> Johnny Cash
> I hear the train a comin'
> It's rolling 'round the bend
> And I ain't seen the sunshine since I don't know when,
> I'm stuck in Folsom prison, and time keeps draggin' on …

I'm sure I would have been a smash hit with that number rather than taking the chance of being smashed on the head. So with head down as far as possible, I was the only escapee that evening (I think).

There were occasions where men slipped away from that jail. I never volunteered to go back there.

During that time, I had learned to play to the interest of my audience. It also broadened my education from the strict classics to other forms of music. I came to love folk music, jazz, and rock and roll and began to listen to the words of country music. Donna expressly loved country-western songs with words that meant so much to her.

For some friends, I would take a basic tune and convert the style according to the great masters, be it Bach, Beethoven, Brahms, Mendelsohn, or Liszt. For others, I would write parodies and at times adaptations of a whole play for fraternity functions. For the old folks, it was ethnic music, be it English, Scotch, Irish, Yiddish, Russian, Spanish, Polish, or German folk tunes. Ach du Lieber, I was a one man show.

But yet, there I was at the piano, void of conversation and sometimes overpowered by the din and active socialization going on. It was still the piano and me. I confess I was a reluctant and shy performer. I wanted to be a part of the greater group and learn about socialization (girls), until dear Mama and later on in life Donna said, "Joel, please play," and so play I did always. I remember once at a family reunion with people gathered around the piano, I played for four straight hours, ending up with sheer exhaustion and a body temperature of 102.6 F.

At age twelve, I became a youth soloist with the Chicago Symphony Orchestra. The classical piano was my instrument, and it suited me well as a soloist in life as well as in music. Music did in retrospect fill my soul and for every emotion, I was able to create a fitting melody. I often wondered if I had continued with this career, could I have been a successful composer and lyricist like George Gershwin, Irving Berlin, or Marvin Hamlisch? I have a way with words but didn't have the sense and fortitude to continue on and pursue this romantic career ... Hollywood never came to me, nor did I chance it. One can say that I quickstepped my way through this phase of life. It reminds me of the song:

Without a Song
by Vincent Youmans

Without a song, the day would never end
Without a song, the road would never bend
When things go wrong, a man ain't got a friend
Without a song.

I was at one point practicing eight hours per day. Our landlady was not exactly a fan, and she would send her boys down (famous lawyers and judges now) asking me to cease and desist. If only they had sent their youngest daughter down, as she was very hot and quite flirtatious and perked up my hormones. You see, I had the right tools, but they were getting rusty.

Here is a funny story about music and hormones. In later years, I collaborated with others to create the annual roast of the Michael Reese Hospital attending physicians. I did this for many years. One year, when the dress rehearsal was over, I was left alone to collect the scores and my music. With this accomplished, I exited through an auditorium door that I had not used before. I was never good at knowing my directions. Were Donna here, she would readily attest to that. The door shut and automatically locked. Guess what. I had sauntered into the nursing school student residence. Looking down (and up more than once in a while!), I quickly exited the residence accompanied by twitters and a few leers. Escorted out through the front door, out into the cold air to cool off, I had to backtrack to the hospital.

I continued to play the piano for many years until the age of computers destroyed my dexterity, and with a trigger finger to boot, I said good-bye to the child prodigy and thus became a mundane aging performer.

As I grew into teenage years, I wanted to do what other fellows did and enter into sports. Upon entering the baseball arena, I instantly developed a baseball finger, a great emancipator and a physical trophy for me. Who could play the piano now? My mom wasn't too happy, as I was her prodigy and her dream child, of whom she was very proud. I became a pretty good first baseman in our pickup games. I then dared to go bowling while Mama warned me about the bad element in these halls of ill repute. Was she the spirit behind the play *Seventy-Six Trombones*? I, however, remember an incident when, with inappropriate bowling skill, I swung too far back. The ball slipped, and on the back swing, I hit my friend Burt square on the noggin. Who knew about concussions or that dreaded word *attorney at law*? One did not sue a friend. We laughed about it once he returned to normal cognition.

Later on in another ill-fated sports attempt, I was playing basketball, making a full-court drive basket—of course for the other team. They won by my two points. My best sport was tennis, and I did admirably well until I ruptured my heel cords (Achilles' tendons) much later on in life.

I was doing a fast dance through life, learning card games, pool ball, and bowling and nervously thinking of girls. As Marty in the song by Frank Loessers said, I was:

> Standing on the corner
> Watching all the girls go by
> Standing on the corner
> Watching all the girls go by ...

But this was not what I wanted in my life. A 180-degree turn in direction and a new career was bringing me closer to Donna. It's funny, but fate played a role in bringing us closer.

Chapter 8

....

Early Years in Medicine

Once I loved such a shattering physician,
Quite the best-looking doctor in the state.
He looked after my physical condition,
And his bedside manner was great.

—"The Physician" by Cole Porter

I do not wish to extol my career as a member of the medical profession, even though that is the point where I first met Donna, as a medical student in 1953 ongoing until we were married and then as a hospital doctor in training and ultimately as a successful physician. When I retired, I left behind a huge practice and a large number of adoring patients who may not have loved me but did love my compassion mixed with well-honed skills. The compassion was a natural transition, as music was my first love and taught me a great deal.

Music is an emotion that always swelled my being. My father always said that my personality must be the balm that heals. From a more practical standpoint, growing up, I considered myself a pianist, but the pyramid to reach the top was quite steep. My last teachers said to go for it but be prepared to end up as a teacher, not a nationally known concert musician.

That convinced me to try something else, so in my late teens, I entered a premedical curriculum. Somewhere about this time is where my love for music and medicine gave way to the love of my life—my wife-to-be. I will shortly tell you how we first met.

I was in premedical school at the University of Illinois, Chicago campus, which was then at Navy Pier. There were several notables who schooled there as well.

To name a few:

In journalism, literature, and writing (from University of Illinois Archives):

- Charles Blackstone, novelist, editor, and winner of the Barker Award for Fiction in 2001

- Patricia Brieschke, PhD, 1983, short-story writer

- John Chancellor (Navy Pier), 1950, leading news anchor for *NBC Nightly News* from 1970 to 1982

- Michael Collins, PhD, 1997, Irish novelist and international ultradistance runner

- Tina de Rosa (master's degree in English), author of *Paper Fish*

- M. Miriam Herrera, MA, 1981, author and poet

- Ma. Luisa Aguilar Igloria, PhD, 1995, Poet and author of various award-winning collections

- Stuart Kaminsky, 1957, author of over fifty award-winning novels, predominantly in the mystery genre

- Rich King, weekend sports anchor and sports reporter for WGN-TV in Chicago

- Gerald Nicosia, BA, 1971, MA, 1973, freelance journalist, interviewer, and literary critic

- Bernard Shaw, 1968, leading news anchor for CNN from 1980 to his retirement in 2001

In medicine and dentistry:

- Mark Frey, BA, 1977, president and chief executive officer, Alexian Brothers Health System

- Stanley J. Korsmeyer (1951–2005), oncologist who helped develop the concepts of the role of programmed cell death in carcinogenesis

- Harry Watson Martin (1889–1951), medical director of 20th Century Fox Studios and third husband of Louella Parsons

- John Short, BS, 1977, senior VP, chief operating officer, Resurrection Medical Center at Resurrection Health Care

- Sheila Tlou, 1990, Botswana specialist in HIV/AIDS

The list goes on and on. It was a very rigorous environment, without frills, filled with educational opportunity and the occasional lamprey eel and fish that washed up into our classrooms during Lake Michigan storms. We called it Harvard on the Rocks. From there, I entered the University of Illinois Medical School on the west side of Chicago.

I was left-handed (always though in my right mind) and was always kicked out of the operating room by the premier surgeon at the medical school because I did not set his operative table right.

One time, while observing a bone marrow aspiration, a robust, red-cheeked healthy pal of mine passed out. Not me! Actually, I found this procedure quite interesting, and it helped me shape my early career in the study of the blood elements.

The night before graduation, we were feasted royally at a well-known hotel. We retired early with expectation for the next day's graduation proceedings. But, wait, thousands were being graduated, one by one and two by two (as in Noah's Ark), when finally, a rush of us medical school graduates raced to the loo (Sir Crapper's invention) needing it desperately! I would say to a man (and woman) we all disappeared in desperation, but fortunately, we recovered in time to get our diplomas (an alternative career would have been a plumber or in the case of *No Time for Sergeants*, permanent latrine orderly).

There was always business to deal with in the emergency room, such as religious Holy Rollers who were in frenzy and plenty of gunshot wound victims. Donna, mostly, and other invited guests would join me there to keep me company. On one particular night with Donna in attendance, I was asked to handle a gunshot wound where a guy said he shot his own finger off. Being a seasoned history taker, I asked the obvious question: "How did it happen, and who did it, sir?" (polite me). He looked at me with drunken eyes and said he was cleaning his gun (I guess it needed cleansing in the outdoor air and a convenient body for further cleansing). The next comment was a mistake. I said I that didn't believe it. With that, he called me something like a four-eyed geek (I wore glasses and didn't have an optical anomaly). He then got up, drew out another weapon, and proceeded to attack me. Donna screamed, the nurses screamed, but the most practical help came from the police officer who had brought him in. He shoved the guy aside.

The Hospital—Safety for Patients? And Once Again, Poor Me

I interned with a huge guy who had played football for Old Miss. This was 1958. This man was a mountain and a lover of raw onions, which he ate every night even when on duty. When he, a very nice guy but oh so intimidating to the ill, walked into a room, you could hear the screams of "Oh No!" and smell the palpable fear mixing with the onions. Many a time, we had to act on his behalf and the patients' need for reassurance. By the way, he became an orthopedic doctor (you can say he was well casted—all puns intended, of course).

Another young brilliant doctor who became a well-known cardiologist in his early days of training was doing a glucose-tolerance test. He missed a vein, and the sugar was infiltrating the soft tissue. Instead of stopping the test and thinking of the patient's cries of discomfort, he sat down and figured out a way to measure the result from soft tissue to bloodstream. Brilliance is not the only ingredient to the making of a physician.

The hospital had a lot of citizens of Romani (Gypsies) and others who after receiving their care from a surgeon in those days would have the bill for services put under their pillow or left at the bedside. I can attest to this, as I was there when people would tie the bedsheets together, climb down from their room, and disappear over the neighboring rail tracks.

But wait, there is more. I was scrubbed in with a neurosurgeon doing a delicate, perhaps futile, operation on a patient, the Queen Gypsy. The patient I noticed had a large gathering just outside of the operating room. The good doctor asked me to inform the clan that the Queen Mother had died. You can guess what happened. At that moment, not only one knife but many appeared with the intent to avenge their loss on my hide. I made a hasty retreat back through the operating room doors, taking the time to glare at my neurosurgeon, who was busily looking elsewhere. Ah the glory of being a doctor! All of the above occurred during my internship in 1958.

There are many more stories but allow me just one more. This is after I returned from military service and completed my residency MD program. I remember this to be about 1962. During my first year of practice, Donna had set up a beautiful office for me, with tables, lamps, and current magazines. In those first hours, I had one patient after another appear and thought that my reputation was heralded by the community. There in my conference room, with my pipe well filled (and I thought my cup runneth over with good fortune), one gentleman kept me busy describing the illnesses in his family. I then left to examine the patient whom I can now call culprit number two. When she said good-bye and left the examining room, I accompanied her to the exit from my office. Woe is me! I noticed that everybody was gone and so was everything: my pipe, my tobacco, and all the furnishings—the entire waiting room had been stripped clean. The sons of Romani had struck again. On a serious note, they stole my prescription blanks and especially my narcotic blanks. I soon found that these were distributed within the community to be used illegally. I received a visit from the Feds and was cleared of any blame. They warned me that this band of criminals went from new (naive) doctor to new doctor employing their skills.

From these stories, you can say live and learn—*learn* being a very cogent term.

Part 2

At Last The Real Dance Begins

Butterfly on Flower

Donna Enters the Stage Full-Time

Chapter 9

· ·

How I Met My Soul Mate

I found my thrill on Blueberry Hill
On Blueberry Hill, when I found you
The moon stood still on Blueberry Hill
And lingered until my dreams came true …
—"Blueberry Hill," composers Vincent Ross and
Larry Stock

It wasn't exactly Blueberry Hill, and blueberries don't grow on hills. It was a fraternity rush party held in a basement of a home. Donna's uncle Joe belonged to this particular fraternity. Uncle Joe's wife, Helen, invited her niece (namely my future spouse) to come and meet some fellas. That was my first glimpse of her. But alas, as the evening progressed, another guy who had a car offered to drive her home. I, for some reason, felt a kind of loss, one that I never felt with my usual encounters with girls. I rushed home and told my parents that I had met this girl I was attracted to. My description was completely off base. I described her as blond with blue eyes. But in fact my wife-to-be had light-brown hair and beautiful hazel eyes. It's a good thing my medical observations during my long career were far more accurate.

I didn't see Donna for a while, as she was busy with the guy who drove her home. Later on, I heard that he was very serious and brought her home to see his parents. I never questioned Donna as to why she did not accept that proposal. It's an interesting thing about that fellow; he turned out to be one of our lifetime friends after he settled on and married another girl. Both he and his wife went out with us many times over the years, and at times, we traveled together. We shared certain things in common, including our children. Each of us had two boys and a girl, and they were all adopted.

Anyhow, the next time I saw Donna was at a play called the *Man from La Mancha*. Donna had fixed me up with her girlfriend. I must confess there was something in me that longed to be near Donna. I left my seat during intermissions to seek out my friend and my future wife. Life plays some interesting tricks on all of us. The girl I was with eventually was married to a wonderful man, and they also became lifetime friends.

What comes to mind as I end this chapter is an old song "The Tennessee Waltz." Some of you may remember these lines.

> I was dancing with my darling to the Tennessee waltz.
> When an old friend. I happened to see.
> I introduced him to my loved one and while they were dancing
> My friend stole my loved one from me.

Whoever reads this book, please don't take this literally. There wasn't much room for dancing in that basement. In addition, my friend did steal Donna away. But as the powers decreed, it was but a short time in the longer road ahead.

"Que Sera Sera"
Composers Ray Evans and Jay Livingston

Que Sera Sera whatever will be will be
The future's not ours to see
What will be will be ...

I guess that is one way of looking at life. Sometimes, I believe this is so.

It was a very rocky road for some time. Donna had another relationship and was about to marry a man who owned a store in another Illinois town. Whether fate played a part or not, I'll never know. Donna never went through with that marriage.

Do any of you remember the movie *A Stranger among Us*, starring Melanie Griffith, who was going undercover in a community of Hasidic Jews? She becomes interested in a man who was waiting for his bashert.

Bashert is a Yiddish word, which means "soul mate," a person considered to be predestined or ideal as a lifetime mate. That is my feeling today. Knowing how life turned out, I believe that Donna was my bashert, who was destined to be with me to share our lifetime together. So in a sense, "Que Sera Sera" also means the same to me as what was to be came to be.

A dear friend and classmate attending a wedding told me that Donna was available again. Though I did not show any outward emotion, my inner self jumped with joy. I did call Donna and began a courtship. This was not like any other idle dating. I knew I was in love with this girl, but just finishing medical school with an internship and specialty training to deal with was overwhelming, as overwhelming as my shyness around girls. In truth, I was a slow worker, and Donna was a patient person with me. I would call her every six weeks or so or for fraternity affairs. But there was something about her that was quite different. There are some things that are not describable—it was her total being. I started to call her on the phone, which was unique for me but it felt so fulfilling. Things heated up and soon we were seeing each other often. I remember our dates, taking a ride along Sheridan Road all the way to distant suburbs. I also remember that she would come to my home to visit with me as I studied. On occasion, I also spent time in her home, and when her parents were not around, we would do what all young couples did in those days. There was a lot of cuddling, kissing, and sitting together under a blanket listening to some old 45 records. One record I remember became the theme song of our life. It was called "Love Is a Many-Splendored Thing." As we were listening to this and snuggled together in her folks' den, I swear she popped the question by saying, "Joel, does this mean we're engaged?" What could I do? I loved her madly but was still this shy guy with golden hands but some problem making my tongue work as fast as my fingers. Since I played the piano, I had many occasions to play this song for Donna during our lifetime. Many of those times were close to the end of her time on earth.

After that was established and sealed within our hearts, parents met parents and we got to know each other's family. I remember my grandmother falling in love with Donna, as did my parents. There is another incident I will always remember. I was in the process of getting Donna an engagement ring, and finally, it was selected. My grandfather was in our dining room at home when my mom and aunts went through the process of trying on their rings to get her ring size. My grandfather with a grin on his face suddenly turned to Donna and said, "Don't worry, child; you are getting your own ring." We all laughed at that.

As life turned out, during our engagement, Grandpa had an accident when visiting a daughter in Milwaukee. Mistaking the basement door for a bathroom door, he fell into the basement and developed a severe head injury and a blood clot in his brain. This could easily have been operated upon, but my grandmother and family were opposed to surgery. He then spent several years as an invalid with severe cognitive decline. This meant that he could not be at our wedding. I guess through the years, one learns that life brings sadness and sorrow as well as joy. I have to interrupt this story meant to be about my soul mate to tell you a side tale. My grandfather was primarily in a comatose state, and during his terminal days, he was hospitalized where I was serving my internship and further training. Late one night, I walked into his room, and suddenly, his eyes opened. He looked at me and began to speak in a logical fashion. I felt that a miracle had occurred and spent many minutes speaking with him. This was not a long-term miracle, as an hour later, he passed away. I will always treasure those last moments with him as experienced only by me.

Chapter 10

· ·

The Bells Are Ringing

Love and marriage—Love and marriage.
Go together like a horse and carriage.
This, I tell you, brother.
You can't have one without the other.
—"Love and Marriage," composers Sammy Cahn
and Jimmy Van Heusen

September 16, 1956, was indeed our beguine. We had a lovely wedding, provided by our parents, and a honeymoon in sunny Florida. Of course, we had lives of our own before this important date, but they were humdrum. This was the beginning of our life together and the slow and easy dance that was to follow for many years to come.

After the wedding, our parents joined us at the airport. This, of course, is not unusual. But what was unusual was an uncle of mine who made up his mind to call us on our first wedding night.

We stayed at a hotel that took up a whole block on Collins Avenue between Thirty-First and Thirty-Second Streets. A hotel by that name is no longer standing. There are now condo buildings in its place.

Anyhow, my funny uncle did call, and we went along with his humor, as well as his instructions. He may have been the first dirty old man that I ever came into contact with. But he was a good soul, and chemistry was his profession, so I didn't want to mix it up with him. (That's a joke, folks.)

By the way, on our honeymoon, every hotel employee looked at us, leered, and said, "Newlyweds, huh?" I was kind of embarrassed, but my Donna "Madonna," if you please, smiled through it all. Donna was never a drinker, but on that first evening, I enticed her during a torrid rhumba to imbibe some rum and cola. I do remember that Donna, a nondrinker, didn't find the drink so bad and enjoyed a few too many. My medical skills were not as yet well-honed as a fledgling medical student, and on top of that, I was an anxious person. (That is an understatement for those who know me.) What a disaster for her and for us, as her subsequent illness, compounded by the uncle's telephoned instructions, led to a less-than-optimal evening of romance. She did sleep it off and was fine for the rest of the trip. We did all the usual things, such as Sea World, Parrots Jungle, swimming, and eating while holding hands and enjoying each other in what we as Northerners considered an exotic area.

When we got home, the fun began. We had to find an apartment to live in and then fill it with some furnishings. We did get a lot of wedding gifts, which took care of our kitchen needs as well as dishes, stemware, etc. We found an apartment at 6969 N. Wolcott in Chicago. The rent was eighty-five dollars per month. Believe it or not, I found this costly, as I had little income as a medical student. Donna, however, had a job nearby at a commercial school that offered varied courses. This was all done by mailings and paper-bound training manuals and testing, not like today where one can find and gain a degree through the Internet just by going online.

Donna's mom lived close by, and while I was in medical school in that first year of our marriage, she would join her mom for lunch every day.

I remember our apartment was on the third floor, and as I was asthmatic, it caused some huffin' and puffin' for me. In those days, I always carried a rescue inhaler just to climb up those three stories. We had a very tiny kitchen with no space for a table. I was never good at building things but was very proud when I put together a hinged wooden device that would pull up when we wished to have a cup of coffee or breakfast. As a wedding gift, we also received a card table and chairs from the father of one of Donna's friends, Fran, a.k.a. "Dixie."

Both sets of parents wished to go with us and pick out some furniture. We were adamant about doing this for ourselves. We went to this furniture store and chose a large, oversized orange chair. Both of us insisted that it was a beautiful piece of furniture. "Not so!" chorused the four parents. I guess when compared with the bridge chairs in our living room, it was certainly the center of attraction. Eventually, we also purchased a small dining room table and chairs. Of course, we had a bed, which would come in handy for Donna—a story soon to be told.

I was never much of a cook, as my grandmother and mother took care of that. However, coming home one day from medical school, I wanted to surprise the breadwinner of our family. I went about preparing a tuna casserole, which I put together, remembering to a degree how my mom prepared it. Much to my surprise, it was pretty darn good. I never prepared a dish again, as I discovered the masterful skills of my wife. Let us just say that these skills, which she learned from her mom, became the talk of all of our friends and relatives. In later years, everyone loved to come to Donna's home and enjoy the festive way in which she prepared a meal for our guests. It was a form of artistry, joining with all her other skills. You will hear this from a neighbor and dear friend later on.

It was probably in my first year of residency at my hospital when I got a frantic call from Donna. "There's a mouse in the house, and I am frightened!" she said. In those days, I had to stay at the hospital when on call and had a room that I shared with a manic-depressive pathologist. I asked her where the mouse was, and she said it was behind the radiator in the bedroom. I then asked her where she was, and she told me on the bed. Now, mind you, I had to travel from this south-side hospital to our home on the north side of town. But I did so after having a buddy cover for me, as this marital commitment for my damsel in distress was most important to me. When I got home, I chased the little *fledermaus* (field mouse) all over the house. I did not want to kill it, so my weapon was a straw broom. I opened up our back porch door and played field hockey with the poor rodent, my primary goal being the eviction of a live critter from our home and saving my damsel in distress. It was a successful play, and all was well. We kissed and flushed with victory. I returned to the hospital and my so-called room. The crazy pathologist that evening had two oil paintings on my bed, two nurses he was entertaining, and a kayak to boot. He was in his manic phase. I retreated to the safer confines of the hospital and slept on some couch or chair.

Our family frequently visited us and may have been the cause of our first argument. I honestly don't remember what it was about or who started it, but I remember us chasing each other around the dining room set. It was probably about which set of parents would have us over for a given holiday. We didn't think of some mutual agreement or maybe having everyone together for the holidays. I also remember that it didn't last too long, and, as we did through the years, we forgave each other. Her father had told us never to go to bed angry.

Aside from family, we often had my medical school buddies come over. In those days, there was a program at midnight that specialized in folk music. It was called *The Midnight Special*. The rest of the time, we played board games and with two special couples created a small movie, simulating the birth of a baby—typical medical school humor. What a grand time those days were.

There is a fun story here. One day, I decided to make the bathroom throne quite regal. (Y'all know what I am referring to, right?) I went out and bought a can of gold paint, and it really looked good. It was slow-drying paint in those days. Within an hour or so, we had a surprise visit from one of Donna's former roommates from when she went to school at the University of Illinois downstate (Champaign-Urbana). Her friend's husband, as fate would have it, had a crisis and asked to use our bathroom. I think it was something about the number that comes after one. I can well imagine the "ring of gold" that adorned him in an unusual place. When they left, Donna and I giggled through the rest of the day and reminisced about it for many years. It's a funny thing, but we never heard from them again. I wonder why …

We stayed in this apartment for several years during my internship and part of my residency until Uncle Sam called upon me to serve my country.

Chapter 11

· ·

The Army Goes Rolling Along

"The Army Goes Rolling Along"

VERSE: First to fight for the right,
And to build the nation's might,
And the Army goes rolling along
Proud of all we have done,

The song was originally written by Field Artillery First Lieutenant (later Brigadier General) Edmund L. Gruber, while stationed in the Philippines in 1908 as "The Caisson Song." The original lyrics reflect routine activities in a horse-drawn field artillery battery. The song was transformed into a march by John Philip Sousa in 1917 and renamed "The Field Artillery Song." Eventually, it was renamed "The Army Goes Rolling Along."

I am very confident that the army will keep rolling along. But at this point in time, Donna and I were rolling on a wonderful adventure called marriage. At the end of my first year of residency, I was called into the medical corp to serve my country. This was in the year 1961.

Let me explain the Berry Plan. The Berry Plan deferred doctors who were taking their residency, so that the army would get the benefit of their advanced education. Those medical corp officers who did not elect option 1 or who were not needed immediately were deferred. Some were allowed option 3, to complete their residency training and then enter active duty as a fully trained specialist. Those who were deferred for only one year of residency were termed "partially trained specialists" and were usually given military assignments that allowed them to work within their specialty. This was my lot. I could not choose my branch of service. It was the army "Mr. Jones"—or should I say, "Dr. Levin"? My best friend at the time was recruited into the air force.

We were now off to basic training in Texas. The training area was called Camp Bullis, a short distance from San Antonio. Of course, we saw the Alamo and ate Southwestern cooking. Donna did not like Mexican food—she really did not like exotic foods (Chinese didn't count)—and oh my, we both received multiple shots, as Donna was going to be with me, wherever that was to be. We both were very sore and had mild fevers for several days. While in basic training, I had to do all the things soldiers did, like using the stars as my guide or an instrument to find my way back after a trainer dropped me off in a forest somewhere. May I say, I was able to get back to camp as the last (more accurately lost) soldier but only when they came looking for me. I had to also crawl under live machine-gun fire. Now you all probably know that Texas is full of rattlers, if you have watched any Westerns in your time. I couldn't decide which ending would be mine—the live bullet or the angry snake—but I made it.

When training was over and graduation day arrived, there was to be a big parade in the quadrangle. You can guess who was honored as the group leader. So I crisply sounded out my commands and marched so elegantly in my uniform. The only trouble was the platoon went one way and I went another. Does that define a klutz or a civilian soldier? Once I made a quick recovery, all was right again except for the good-natured kidding, with my wife giggling. When we watched *MASH* on television, it brought back the humor of the situation.

Finally, basic training was over, and we were asked where we would like to serve. I was enchanted with the crisp and clean white uniforms worn in Panama, so that was my first choice. I next chose an area in the United States, just any place where there was a large hospital. It really made no difference. This was the time of the Cold War with the then USSR. When the list came out, most of us were sent to Germany. It was quite a shock for us, but can you imagine the shock to our collective parents? I heard that my dad called his congressman asking that I be relieved of this duty. How embarrassing! But in retrospect, I understand their fear of our going to that country so soon after World War II and of course the Holocaust.

With this news in hand, we rushed back home and actually got back within twenty-four hours. There was the whole family on both sides waiting up to all hours to see us. It was bittersweet. I felt for them, but in a way, we were excited. We said our good-byes, not realizing that certain things would happen during the two years we were away. I said fare thee well to Donna, as I had to leave on a military air transport plane, and she was to meet me several weeks later. Dependent wives could not travel on military aircraft. I hated to leave her, of course, and the parting for us was sad. I had to sit backward in an army aircraft (MAT), as they felt this was safer. The first stop was Greenland, where the ice along the airstrip seemed two stories high. We were held up because the engines were frozen and one had to be changed. Our next stop was Shannon, Ireland, and then the final leg of the journey was Frankfurt, Germany.

My assignment was to the military hospital in Frankfort, Germany. What a surprise awaited me. When I arrived, there was a Sergeant W., who saluted me, and said, "Right this way, Captain."

I said, "The hospital is right here. Where are we going?"

The reply was that I was assigned to the military dispensary in Gelnhausen, Germany. This was at least forty kilometers west of the hospital assignment I longed for. The good news was that I was to be the medical director of this facility and would be in charge of the dependents, not the soldiers. This dispensary was part of the Third Armored Division, Second Brigade, US Army in Europe. When we arrived, I was introduced to all the personnel and to doctors in charge of the soldiers. I also saw that my mode of transportation would be an army ambulance. I knew that I would have to bring my car over to Germany.

Donna arrived by commercial airline, and I met her in Frankfort with great relief. It was good to have my mate right next to me. Donna and I had arranged to send along several items, including my stereo setup. We also sent for my Chevy and had to go to the port city of Bremerhaven to pick it up. What a mistake. Here was this huge Sedan with large fin tails, and we were living in rural Germany in the heart of small towns and narrow, winding roads. We quickly transitioned into a more-suitable 1959 Volvo.

Donna and I had to live on the economy, as I had not agreed to serve for the three years necessary for government housing. We went searching and found a place in a neighboring tiny village called Altenhauslau. We met our landlords-to-be, Frau and Herr Friedrich, themselves émigrés from the Sudetenland in Czechoslovakia. Somehow,

Frau F. knew the exact housing allowance, so there was no discussion or room for negotiation.

A description of our home away from home is not to be believed. It was an attic with a sloping roof in the tiny living room. There was no central heating or water. The living room had a coke burner, the tiny kitchen a small electric device that would heat the water, and the shower had a device that needed oil to warm the water. For two middle-class kids, this took a little adjustment. Frau F. would come up every evening to light the coke burner and tuck us in under a downdecken cover. She was really a very nice lady and her husband, a very humble man. Our house was on a muddy road that was unpaved, so during a rainstorm or the rainy season, which was almost always, they would clean my military shoes. Donna's shoes were also always sparkling clean.

My stereo set was my pride and joy, and I knew that there was a difference in the current requirements between Europe and the United States. I purchased the appropriate transformer and began to set up the stereo set. Of course, you know what happened. Within one minute, the entire set blew up and was totally gone forever. Donna was a little luckier with her possessions, which were basic needs, such as dishes and kitchen items. I should mention that much of our furniture in our attic apartment was handmade, including the elegant orange crate side tables and cupboards.

The stereo set was soon replaced with a beautiful German-made all-in-one radio and phonograph manufactured by a well-known German company called Grundig. We had a military store called a PX and over the two years took advantage of it. One could buy food and other essentials there, as well as all kinds of equipment. I bought a beautiful camera there with multiple lenses, as I knew that part of our stay in

Germany would be a grand adventure. I wanted to be sure that I would capture it all with a good camera.

Here is a very interesting association. When I joined the army, guess who else was there. That great idol, that hip-and-pelvis-gyrating guy Elvis Presley was assigned to the Third Armored Division in a different brigade in a neighboring town called Hanau. For those of you who don't know the significance of the town, it was the birthplace of the Grimm brothers, the great storytellers. I never met Elvis, as he was off entertaining the troops. Maybe I could have stepped into his blue suede shoes.

My job was quite interesting, and basically, I was a family physician for two years. I made a lot of nice friends, doing my best to keep military families healthy. Through this association, Donna met some of the officers' and soldiers' wives. This kept her occupied, as she spoke no German. The other advantage was she could visit her new friend Bernadette, the wife of an army officer. She was always welcome to use her Laundromat machine. Bernadette and Donna became great friends and in later years still kept in touch. Sadly, we heard several years later, in the late 1960s, that her dear husband had passed away Stateside. We also had a lot of other friends, including the dispensary doctors and their wives and a pharmacist and his wife. This allowed us many hours of pleasant conversation and improvement of our bridge-playing expertise. We were quite timid about going into town alone without these friends. Most of the good German food was in Frankfurt, Germany, and we took advantage of that. There was also a famous café called the Kranzler Café, where delicious Viennese pastries were available. I don't remember many of the city sites we visited, but pastries stick in my mind and of course did the same to my belly. I was still young and in good shape, as

I was able to fit into my uniform and fatigues comfortably despite the rich pastries and the famous German Schartzbrot.

There were occasions when an army wife was in labor and was too advanced to be sent to the army hospital in Frankfort. I'd had a rotation in obstetrics during my internship. As luck would have it, I delivered several healthy children. The news got around that Dr. Levin was a regular Marcus Welby. Giving it some thought, I set up a small obstetrical unit in our dispensary. And guess who Nurse Nancy was? Donna was enamored with the idea of delivering babies into this world, and she became my assistant. Together, we must have delivered about ten babies during my tour of duty. Let me now add that to the many talents of my dear wife.

Donna had no trouble driving because she was always an excellent driver, but she ran into a few difficult moments. For instance, she would often be caught behind a farmer driving his honey wagon. In passing, let me mention that the honey wagon was filled with fertilizer, which was often animal and human excreta. The farmer, taking his sweet time (bad choice of words), took no notice of the Frau behind him. Now I must tell you that my wife was a very verbal driver, which I always feared would get her into trouble when we came back to the States. I always asked her not to raise her voice or use a certain raised finger gesture. Not speaking German, imagine if she mumbled "Heraus" instead of "Mein Herr Bitte." She could have started the fighting all over again. Or maybe the finger gesture was an international one recognized by the man driving his honey wagon.

Her other challenge was getting caught in the middle of US tanks on convoy. You remember I was in an armored division, and there were plenty of tanks maneuvering this way and that way and often in Donna's way. A last challenge was watching for domestic animals and deer, for the German government was very strict with Americans and imposed very heavy fines. That never happened to her.

Donna did not speak German, as she had been a French student in high school. But she had a smattering of words that helped her get by. She knew *yes* as "ja" and *no* as "nein." She knew *weidersehan*, short for *auf weidersehen* (good-bye or until we meet again) and of course like any woman shopper, "Wie viel kostet es?" (How much does it cost?) or when lunching asking for the bill "Kann ich bitte die Rechnung haben?" She always got by with her smile and charm. Who could resist this foreign Amerikaner with her broken German?

While Donna experienced these things in Germany, I had to go on army maneuvers because the dispensary personnel, like all of the army units, had to go on field maneuvers. Since I was the dispensary commanding officer, it was my duty to lead the troops. Being naive and inexperienced, I put on freshly pressed fatigues, filled my backpack with army rations, and marched our group out of town at a doubletime pace.

When we arrived at the designated area of maneuvers, out came baseball bats, gloves, and softballs. I was prepared to offer these soldiers rigid calisthenics, marching, and lectures in health and medicine but in time succumbed and joined in the games. When it was time to eat, I took out my K rations and heard a bunch of my men laughing. You see, my experienced top sergeant, whose name I remember as Wenzel, had his wife prepare fried chicken topped off with homemade fudge brownies. I quickly learned from Sarge how the army really worked. We returned to the dispensary at a very slow and leisurely pace.

Since many of our dispensary staff members were quite young and away from home, Donna, only a few years older than these boys, decided to make our dispensary festive for the holidays. She went out with one of our young technicians to purchase a tree. Mind you, our dispensary waiting room had a very high ceiling, but this Christmas tree was well beyond it. It needed considerable trimming to allow it to fit in the waiting room. Donna also found many Christmas decorations, and I must admit it was quite beautiful. It brought her much joy to make Christmas as pleasant as possible for the young GIs. We served nonalcoholic punch to our staff and all the patients. This brings up another interesting story. One of the older guys who worked in the dispensary was an alcoholic, and it was my duty to manage him from a military standpoint. But first I had to find his stash. He used to draw blood for laboratory testing and do the electrocardiograms for me. After looking all over, I found his booze supply hidden in a cabinet below the electrocardiogram machine. The man could have been demoted or court-martialed, but being a nonregular army person, I chose to ignore it and always tried very hard to counsel him. You know how hard that can be …

In the army, one hand often washes the other. Such was it with my top sergeant. I let him manage the dispensary, and he let me be the physician. With this arrangement, I was able to have him sign many weekend passes. Not only did we see much of Germany but in one day would arrive in Luxembourg and in a few hours be at the borders of France. We saw many of the beautiful German castles and traveled along the Rhine River. We also visited many places in France. This was the first time we had ever seen Paris, like the song "The First Time I Saw Paris." The weirdest thing I remember was the outdoor, shall we say, *water closets*. We saw many sites, the Eifel Tower, churches (Le Sacre Couer), and of course the nightclubs (Ooh la la). We dined in Parisian restaurants, always getting a back table and enduring the aloofness of the French waiters. Many of them spoke perfect English but refused to acknowledge this and made us suffer trying to decide what to eat. One interesting experience was walking down the Champs-Élysées and passing an outdoor café. To our surprise, we ran into a close friend of Donna's dad's and a man who lived on a street destined to be the street of our future dreams. In our travels, we even got to London, a wondrous place to see. I need not mention all the history in London Town, Westminster Abbey, the Towers of London, and the Parliament. We also visited Stratford-on-Avon, reputedly associated with Shakespeare. We went to the older sections of London and dined in a few pubs. I was always willing to try new foods, like fish and chips and warm ale. Donna was always more cautious.

On my second trip to London, I boarded the small airplanes with maybe sixteen to twenty or more seats for the short flight. I did not like flying, and on this particular trip, I was quite anxious. My wedding ring actually fell off and went rolling down the aisles. I panicked and thought this was the end of the world. I told everybody that if they didn't find the ring, we were all doomed. My ring was soon retrieved, and all was well as we flew across the English Channel and glimpsed the white cliffs of Dover. We actually ate traditional English pub food, and I loved the ale.

In order to see Berlin, we needed a special pass and had to travel on the night train in regular clothes. It was forbidden to travel in uniform. On our way to Berlin, we had to travel through Russian-occupied Germany. We were told to keep the shutters on the train windows down at all times. Being inquisitive, I did sneak a few peeks. What I saw was quite frightening. Russian or East German soldiers with large dogs and weapons were ready at every station along the way. When we did get to Berlin, it was like seeing two extremes. The western part of Berlin, occupied by the Allies, was filled with activity and reconstruction everywhere you looked. It was winter, and I remember the white snow complemented by beautiful blue sky. We visited the university and a famous museum, which housed a sculpture of Queen Nefertiti. When going through the Brandenburg Gate, we had to convert the German mark into eastern currency. We were allowed to travel a short distance along the main road. There were very few people walking about, and the buildings all looked alike, very Soviet style in construction. When one looked very closely, one could see these were merely facades. We were very happy to leave this morbid East Berlin and return to West Berlin and then back to our home away from home.

Things were going well in Germany, and in the second year of my service, we received a message that my mom was coming to visit us. I merely thought that she was lonesome for her kids, and we both looked forward to the upcoming visit. When my mother arrived and we brought her to our attic home, she immediately made friends with our landlords and was able to converse in a form of German that the Friedriches easily understood. I was always amazed by Mom's fluency in so many languages. After we settled in a bit, the reason for her visit became apparent and was a sad one to hear. My beloved grandmother had died that year, and her mission was to give us the news in person. Donna loved my grandmother and vice versa.

With her there, we were in tight quarters, so we decided to travel with her to see some of the sites in Europe. I found an interesting tour that would take us through Germany, Austria, Switzerland, and Italy. The ultimate interest in this tour was a visit to the newly founded state of Israel.

Rome was very interesting, and we saw the ancient structures, like the Colosseum. We actually visited Vatican City and had a group audience with the pope (I believe it was the friendly ecumenical Pope John). We bought crucifixes and beads for all of our Catholic friends and had them blessed by Pope John during our audience. Though Rome was unique, many of the cities in Italy were beautiful and the people quite friendly. From northern Italy and Milan, we traveled to southern Italy and the Isle of Capri. I remember that Donna and I saw an area of activity, and much to our surprise, a movie was being made. There before us stood the king of Hollywood at that time, Mr. Clark Gable.

Lest I forget, I also remember the wondrous talent of Michelangelo exhibited in his sculptures and his frescoes and paintings.

The trip to Israel with a mixed group of different ethnicities was quite interesting. We visited Haifa and were hosted by a well-to-do Arab family. We enjoyed the visit immensely. From there, we traveled along the Mediterranean coast visiting some of the early group settlements, called kibbutzim, and looked at the wonder of this young country turning the desert back into the land of milk and honey. There were orange groves everywhere, as well as palm trees, olive trees, and newly planted forests—all agricultural miracles in desert land. Everybody was hard at work. They may have been professors and doctors in their old homes in Europe, but here, everyone was a laborer of sorts. It was interesting as we traveled to Jerusalem and in mixed company saw Jewish, Christian, and Muslim holy sites. Further south, many of the old cities were archaeological sites and new cities were built upon the ancient structures. I remember dancing with these young pioneers in Ashkelon to the music of the new land and a shepherd's fife. All we could see was a new country being reborn from an ancient Israel. When we reached the southernmost part of our visit and what was the Gaza

Strip, we were greeted by young children throwing stones at us or using slingshots. This is not political, but my comment is that some things never change. Well, maybe technology changed—slingshots became launchers, and stones became rockets. But people stubbornly go along trying to destroy each other as well as Mother Earth.

We were sorry to see Mom leave but knew we would soon be reunited because my tour would be over soon. Little did we know that Donna's mother was quite sick with breast cancer, as this news was kept secret from her and her brothers. That part of the story will follow shortly.

Donna and I were thinking of settling in California, when my tour of duty was over, but that move was never to be realized. My dad, a prolific letter writer, kept telling me how important it was to return to Chicago but did not tell us why. So I informed my chief of medicine that I would be returning to complete my residency in Chicago.

Before my tour was over, Donna was told that her mother was gravely ill with breast cancer, and she had to return to the States as soon as possible. I had to say good-bye to my beloved once again. Once she left, I moved into the BOQ (otherwise known as the bachelor officer's quarters). I had to shift for myself for a month or so before I was to be mustered out of my active service. I missed my wife immensely and became quite introverted when I wasn't busy in the medical dispensary.

The day finally came when I returned to the States. I had to report to Fort Dix, New Jersey, but I arrived in New York City first. I had a rather comical experience with a native New Yorker at the airport. I was in full uniform carrying my duffel bag, which brushed against this gentleman. He said, "Watch out where you're going, buddy." I now know how some of our young soldiers feel today and the veterans of Vietnam felt on their return to the United States. Many of them broken in spirit and tired of war were treated in similar manner, never hearing the words, "Thank you for your service," such as they do today. Anyhow, I had to pick up my car, which by that time had gone from Chevy to Volvo. I now had a sporty version of the Volkswagen called the Kharman Ghia. Speedily driving to New Jersey and Fort Dix, where I was to be mustered out of active overseas duties, I was apprehended by a state policeman and given a speeding ticket. For all I know, I'm still wanted in that state, having never paid the fine.

That car had to be shipped home because my dad, who hated flying as much as I did, decided to greet his son on his return home. He actually white-knuckled it and flew to Philadelphia, where I met him joyously. He informed me of the urgency of our getting home since Donna's mom was near the end of her life's voyage. My father wanted to see me home safely, knowing the truth of the situation. My dad was always a compassionate, caring man, having experienced his own life struggles, losing both of his parents at the young age of forty-five and his kid brother, whom he had to take care of at that same age. Everyone loved Marty, as they used to call him. I arrived home in the nick of time, joining my wife at her mother's bedside as she passed away. There is a curse on that side of the family, having inherited a genetic code that ultimately doomed every maternal aunt or uncle with one sort of cancer or another. Donna always feared that her time would come, and I did all I could to reassure her and protect her from certain medications and hormones, which I felt were contraindicated. I am thankful I had her for fifty-seven years before she was called home. Incidentally, that tumor marker (BRCA 1 and 2) has been passed on to the next generation, and I truly feel sorry for them. These markers are commonly found in Ashkenazi Jews as well as other ethnicities. For my readers, the physician in me wants to explain this further.

Tumor markers are substances found in the blood, body fluids, or tissues that are produced by cancer cells. If a certain tumor marker is found in the body, it can indicate that the cancer is still present and ongoing treatment may still be recommended.

Our oncologists use tumor molecular profiling to:

- identify the unique molecular blueprint of each patient's tumor

- choose cancer treatments that are more likely to be effective and rule out those that are unlikely to be effective on an individual patient basis, minimizing trial and error

- discover potentially beneficial treatment options that may not have been considered in an initial treatment plan

Individual Profiling

Every cancer cell has its own pattern of active genes and proteins. Molecular profiling tests for a variety of biomarkers in the DNA of a tissue sample to help us better diagnose, stage, and treat cancer on an individualized basis.

Consider referencing "Cancer Risk and Genetic Testing" from the National Cancer Institute at the National Institutes of Health.

"How Ya Gonna Keep 'Em Down on the Farm?"
How ya gonna keep em down on the farm after they've seen Paree?

How'ya gonna keep'em down on the farm, after they've
seen Paree?
How'ya gonna keep'em away from Broadway,
Jazzin' aroun', and Paintin' the town?
That's a mystery. (Lyrics by Sam Lewis and Joe Young)

This is an old doughboy song from World War I. In a comical sense, this seems most fitting for this next chapter of our life together. Yes, we had seen Paris several times, and we were going home. We had great expectations of finding our own place and settling down. This is where that great prolific writer, my dad, once again plays a role …

While I was still in service, waiting to be mustered out, and Donna was home with her very sick mother, I received a rather lengthy letter from my father. I knew the truth of the situation and the compassionate nature of my father. He told me that my father-in-law would be all alone and needed someone to keep house for him. It was fate accompli. Our life for the next few years would be shared living with my father-in-law and Donna's younger brother. The other brother had already found a career and moved to Kansas City.

I remember this period of time as a dutiful son-in-law and brother-in-law. I also remember this as a clash between the old physician and the new physician—*moi*. We disagreed on many points but always in a respectful manner. One such area was in feeding young children. He believed in lots of butter mixed into formula. I, of course, was well-versed in the danger of high-fat, high-cholesterol diets. It was a classic example of experience versus evidence-based medicine. Guess who won.

There are a few interesting anecdotes before we leave the old homestead.

As a young doctor, I was making a huge salary of a hundred dollars per month. Moonlighting or seeking other jobs was commonplace, but as a resident physician, it could be dangerous. The medical director considered it a luxury to be a resident doctor in a prestigious hospital, and one could lose this position quite easily and be booted into private practice. I was one of many who had additional jobs, ones that never interfered with our hospital duties. Since my father-in-law had a small office on Morse Avenue in Rogers Park with his shingle hanging above a drugstore, I was invited to help him, especially with house calls. When I had occasion to treat his patients, the entire history of the patient was on an index card. Try to compare that with modern-day record keeping and electronic records.

My father-in-law was not only prominent in his profession but in his habitus. Let us say he was a very solid, well-built gentleman bordering on morbid obesity. He had a very varied practice, being a general practitioner, and actually delivered babies. But can you then guess what his subspecialty was? Yes, my friends, he was a diet doctor. Here is an interesting story. There was a well-known comedian, Shecky Greene, who was a patient of my father-in-law's. When Donna and I were in Vegas years later, we saw that the diet doctor was part of Shecky's routine.

Meanwhile, Donna's father and brother were still living with us. At one point, the brother from Kansas City came to call. He came with a small sporty car and a lady on his arm (I use the term cautiously). This lady had some peculiar habits, such as leaving her laundry in our front room closet. Needless to say, my wife intervened, feeling this to be an unsuitable arrangement for her brother. She asked the young lady to depart (booted her out!). Well, she did depart rather hastily, taking her dirty laundry with her and my brother-in-law's car to boot.

For a young couple, we certainly had a lot to contend with, missing the freedom of our days in military service and recognizing the reality of our then current situation. Not only was she a daughter and wife, she had to take on the role of mother for her youngest brother. She did this knowingly, willingly, and lovingly. I sincerely hope he remembers that period of his life.

Chapter 12

....

Children

M is for the many things she gave me,
O means only that she's growing old.
T is for the tears she shed to save me,
H is for her heart of purest gold.
You remember the rest, I am sure. Put them all
together. They spell mother.
A word that certainly meant the world to me ...
—"M-O-T-H-E-R: A Word that Means the World
to Me" by Theodore F. Morse

Boy, was she a good mom! From the very start of their young lives and throughout the years, she loved and adored the children. Of course, I also played a role, but this story is dedicated to her. I shared in the love and caring. But I had a job to go to. Donna's job was to keep our home safe and sound for her loved ones.

In our early years of marriage, Donna tried to get pregnant. Since we were unsuccessful, we went to a fertility specialist recommended to us. Donna went through exhaustive testing, which culminated in a very painful biopsy. It was much simpler for me to give the doctor a simple specimen in a cup. The answer was soon to be revealed. As a child, I was born with several congenital abnormalities. The analysis was that my donation to making a child was rather weak, and had I known that, Donna would not have had to go through the difficult procedures.

Donna's father delivered babies as a part of his practice, and he also, in many instances, found adoptive parents for the children of unwed mothers or parents who could not afford more children to raise. Out of his love for his daughter, he personally searched for babies whose parents were in good health, both from a physical and mental standpoint. Not only did he go through a selection process, but—get this—he delivered all of these babies that were meant for us. He was not only their grandfather but their obstetrician. For this, I am ever grateful to Grandpa Clarence, may he rest in peace.

Of course adoption requires a legal process, which we went through, and a selection process where we were interviewed. I am thankful that we were found to be worthy of these children. These are the dates our children were born:

Raymond, May 5, 1961
Kenneth, August 24, 1962
Cheryl, September 16, 1964

Cheryl was born on our anniversary, and we had to share that day of celebration for many years.

For my children and many other chosen ones, let's talk about adoption.

By definition, it is an act of transferring parental rights and duties to someone other than the adopted person's biological parents. The practice is ancient and occurs in all cultures. Traditionally, its goal was to continue the male line for the purposes of inheritance and succession; most adoptees were male (and sometimes adult). Contemporary laws and practices aim to promote child welfare and the development of families, but it is an ancient custom. One can go back to Moses and the land of Egypt. During the exodus, all slaves, be they Israelite or of other ancestry, were free to leave and were adopted so to speak by the entire group. In the animal kingdom, maternal instincts prevail and an unrelated mother will raise the children of a deceased mother. Perhaps the most beautiful story is that of Ruth the Moabite. According to the biblical book of Ruth, Ruth was a Moabite woman who married into an Israelite family and eventually converted to Judaism. She is the great-grandmother of King David and hence an ancestor of the Messiah. She again was adopted into Israelite culture.

These famous words are recorded in Judeo-Christian theology. Ruth, speaking to her mother-in-law, Naomi, says: "Intreat me not to leave thee, or to return from following after thee: for whither thou goest, I will go; and where thou lodgest, I will lodge: thy people shall be my people, and thy God my God" (Ruth 1:16 King James Version).

It was fun to come home to "Ma" Donna and children. We were very happy and content being parents. My wife always had a smile on her face in those days. Just recently, my son Ken came home for Father's Day, and we looked through some old pictures. In sequence, it showed all of our children from infancy to their growing up. My wife was very particular in how each child was dressed. Not only were things bought but also made by Donna. She was a great seamstress, great cook, and great mom. Actually, I recall that she did a lot of sewing when we were in the service, and there will be a story to tell about that. Of course, I admit to spoiling all of them, showering them with toys and gifts while Donna did the hard work of raising them. We tried to agree not to disagree, and in retrospect, I recognize she was always right in her decisions. She gave them structure and schedules and fought their battles and their demons throughout their school years, while I brought home the bacon, so to speak. Those were wonderful years, and our relationship as a married couple with children blossomed. Donna loved her buggy walks with each child and meeting her friends and children in the park or at home. I could not wait to get home to see my kids. We were very proud parents.

We took many trips with the children, both locally and in other parts of the United States. We returned to Florida with them several times, staying at the Montmartre, Beau Rivage, and Fontainebleau Hotels. Several times, we were joined by her parents and mine trying to escape the harsh Chicago winters. Later when cruising became fashionable and affordable to us, my mom at times joined us as we cruised to the Caribbean and the west coasts of Mexico and Alaska. What a joyous time we had.

During the summer, we spent a week or so at a resort in Wisconsin for several years. We traveled a lot into Wisconsin, as there were things for families to do together.

Mind you, we were not a father-knows-best-family in all respects, as Donna and I were equal partners. There was none of "wait until your Father comes home." That was to be our equal relationship from the beginning. Our home was a place to be. Our home was always open to all. All the children on our block loved our household and especially the basement with its pool table, pinball machine, and various games. The two boys used the basement as a hockey stadium, banging that awful hard hockey puck against one basement door, which was a bit battered and bruised.

Recently, when I was in rehab for my hip replacement, a young man who is now an administrator of a facility recalled those days of fun. He was one of those kids many years ago. He told me that the Levin place was the place to be at.

All these kids grew up through the 1960s and the revolutions that were happening as well as the fear of a nuclear war. This changed their childhood forever, and their parents' naive security as well. The 1960s were a period when values and norms of behavior seemed to break down, particularly among the young. Many became political activists and were the driving force behind the civil rights and antiwar movements. Other young people simply dropped out and separated themselves from mainstream culture through their lifestyle and the way they dressed. Attitudes toward sexuality appeared to loosen, and women openly protested the traditional roles of housewife and mother that society had assigned to them. This shocked Donna, and many times when she had to fill out forms, she hesitated to say housewife and we would jokingly create a title for her. The hippies, the "flower children," were mostly middle-class whites but without the political drive. Their hallmarks were a particular style of dress that included jeans, tie-dyed shirts, sandals, beards, long hair, and a lifestyle that embraced sexual promiscuity and recreational drugs, including marijuana and the hallucinogenic LSD. Remember Woodstock? The sex and drug culture were reflected in the rock music of the time by such groups as Jefferson Airplane and the Grateful Dead and performers like Jim Morrison and Janis Joplin. I heard these constantly on the radio and even at home. Although some young people established communes in the countryside, the Haight-Ashbury section of San Francisco and the East Village in New York were the focal points of the counterculture for a brief period from 1965 to 1967. This is what our kids grew up with. They also lived through the successive assassinations of President Kennedy, his brother Robert Kennedy, and the Reverend Martin Luther King Jr.

Here is a song that you may be familiar with, "Abraham, Martin and John." This song is a tribute to those involved in the battle for civil rights. The title refers to Abraham Lincoln, Martin Luther King Jr., and John F. Kennedy. The last verse in the song refers to "Bobby," JFK's brother, Robert Kennedy. Everyone mentioned in the song has died ("has anybody here seen my old friend …"), and this is symbolized by their progression over a hill. This has been sung by the Brothers Four, Ray Charles, Kenny Rogers, Marvin Gaye, Smokey Robinson, Mahalia Jackson, and Moms Mabley. It was written by rockabilly singer Dick Holler.

"Abraham, Martin and John."

Anybody here seen my old friend Abraham?
Can you tell me where he's gone?
He freed lotta people but it seems the good they die young
You know I just looked around and he's gone

There was Kent University and other college rebellions, the mayor of one city using ferocious dogs against kids, and a governor not letting innocent black children into a school that was to be integrated. Lest we forget, promiscuity led to the first cases of autoimmune deficiency syndrome in San Francisco. This was also the time of the British Invasion and the Beatles among others (not the kind of beetles invading my yard now, destroying trees and shrubs). Donna and I felt like the saying goes, "Stop the world. I want to get off."

Chapter 13

• •

A Change in the Rhythm of Our Life

The Dance through Life Quickens

Come mothers and fathers throughout the land
Don't criticize what you can't understand
Your sons and your daughters are beyond your
command
Your old road is rapidly agin' …
—Bob Dylan, "The Times They Are A'-Changin'"

As Bob Dylan said, times were changing in the 1960s, and the kids were facing a new world and we had new challenges.

Yes, I always loved folk music, especially the songs of Bob Dylan, and the times they were certainly changing. It was a shock for both Donna and me, growing up in an earlier, easier, less complex time of life. Although there were days of depression and war, families and communities stood solidly together as they had for many generations.

We found that many of our combined families had relocated to different cities in different states or did not wish to keep up relationships. This hurt Donna immensely, and for years, she tried to keep the remaining family together, always opening our home during holidays or just for togetherness with family and friends. She was a consummate hostess, and when our parents died, she took over that hospitality chore. This was sometimes successful but not always so. One of her brothers had moved away, and the other younger brother had his own life to lead. She tried very hard to stay loyal to them. As to the next generation of nephews and nieces, there was little to no contact during her later years.

As our children grew, problems grew also. Donna and I had a solid relationship, and if there was any dynamic issue, it was how we handled our kids. One can say we started to bicker somewhat, as I was not always home to see situations evolving and Donna was there at all times. I guess you can say I was more permissive and she was stricter. I'm not going to go into detail about their problems in later adolescent years, as it is not my plan in this memoir to shame them or blame them. I continue to love them as much as their mom did. It is just factual to our life story. They had some difficult times growing up, and so did we, having to grow and change, but we all made it, thank God! They had a very different world to grow up in, and they were not much different from many children of their generation.

At times, things were distressing for both of us. We were angered by all that was happening, and in truth, there were times we saw things differently and from opposite perspectives. We even started to argue about child rearing, and although the situation was at times perplexing and difficult, the fiber of our marriage was sound. I put the following thought together during this period of our life because some of the things I did were wrong and I knew it. Donna, at that time, was more consistent, and I think she helped me see the correct approach. It led to the following honest inventory

True Love without Conditions

To love a child is more than a kiss
It takes more than money can buy
You must listen and learn when things are amiss.
And not waste your time yesterday.

Anger and hate will a family divide.
What you think you have gained will be lost.
The hurt inside and that injured pride
Must be traded no matter the cost.

Let one thought rule, play not the fool
And think of how things could have been.
Above all, stay cool, let serenity rule.
Let reason prevail from within.

We're not the potter who molds the clay
Or the weaver, who works at the loom.
We cannot control what they do or say.
Let them grow and mature, give them room.

This love that I speak of is hard to attain.
One must learn not to stand in the way.
They have to experience those troublesome storms
As well, as the sunshiny days.

True love then is not to enable or soothe.
Or to threaten and strike with your wrath.
It isn't our task to make the road smooth
But rather suggest a new path.

To my Power, I'll listen, till I get the knack
And not have my own thoughts run wild.
My earnest prayer is to get on the track.
Of true love for my child.

The following is from Carol King's "Child of Mine."

Although you see the world different than me
Sometimes I can touch upon the wonders that you see
All the new colors and pictures you've designed
So glad you are a child of mine.

This refrain means a lot to me. The times got rougher as the children grew, and we had to get tougher. But before the maelstrom hit and everything seemed well, I would like to once again share an original poem. Donna referred to periods in her life as quarters. This would be the second quarter, when we had settled into a comfortable lifestyle, and this is how we felt:

I'll tell you a story of which there's no doubt,
the Lord said one day, there's no children about
So pray very hard, lift up your voice,
And soon will appear God's very own choice

And so we prayed and waited each day
Our first choice from heaven arrived as a Ray

A ray of the sun to carry our name.
We had so much love, so his second choice came

As sweet as sugar, so perky a boy.
God gave his Kenneth, our second great joy,
The day of your birth, we cherish each day.
A blessing from heaven, a joy sent our way

With two fine boys, we both had such bliss.
But God had a third choice, he sent us a miss.
One look at her eyes, one look at that smile.
The third choice a miniature Donna in style.

And now we were happy with our children three
No doubt God chose each one of the three.
Each night when they slept, a night never missed
When slumber is deepest, their foreheads we kissed.

Children on this day and all days to be.
There's nothing that matters more for Mother and me.
Our wish and our hope for each one of you.
Please choose to love us, as we love you.

This was written August 24, 1969. Though Donna is now gone and I am left to speak for both of us, we still mean it to this day. We wanted you, we loved you, and we did the best we could.

People are all so different, even in one's own family. Let me quote something from a book of poems collected by Donna's mother. It is called "Cataloging the Family" by Elizabeth Elsie Zileh.

People, they say are flesh and blood
But I beg to disagree
That they can be inanimate
Is evident to me

Chapter 14

Jarlath at Last

The town I live in,
The street, the house, the room,
But especially the people;
That's America to me.
—Abel Meeropol, "The Town I Live In"

This became a patriotic anthem in America during World War II. The lyrics describe the wonderful things about the country, with images of the era like the grocer, the butcher, and the churchyard. The "house" is a metaphor for the country.

Old Blue Eyes had another song about Chicago and that great street State Street. Oh yes, we loved the city, its lights, its people, and the many things to do. And as that song went, I even danced with my wife. We loved to dance and did so for many years until her arthritis began to take a toll. I'm sure there was a hereditary component, as her dad suffered with the same malady. As a child growing up in the early 1940s, I told you that she developed polio and this left her with a very badly deformed ankle. In addition to this, my wife had several falls over the years. I must relate an interesting story. Since she was not an athlete and never wanted to play tennis or golf with me but was more on the artistic side, she never had a sports hobby. I had encouraged her to join a local gym, and she agreed to do so. The very first time she tried to strengthen her knees with the health club apparatus, it gave way and fell directly onto one of her knees. That was basically the end of her athletic endeavors, but she had so much else going for her, that wonderful lady of mine.

Let us now return to the story about Jarlath Street, that great street. I once looked it up and found that our street was named after Saint Jarlath (sixth century), an Irish priest and scholar. How we ever found this street, which ran for a few blocks, may be of some interest. How we needed to find this street is another story.

All three of our children were born on Lunt Avenue in Chicago a few blocks away from Lunt Beach and Sheridan Road. It was in 1965 that my father-in-law had remarried and with his new wife wanted to move into a larger condominium. He needed to sell his house and informed us as such. When I heard the news, it was my intent to look for a home in the suburban areas, assuming that the school system might be better. We looked at several homes, but none seemed satisfactory. I am sure fate played a role in this.

At the time, I was a young resident physician at Michael Reese hospital, and we had an outreach program to various neighborhoods. I was given my assignments and one of those was to see an elderly couple living with their son and daughter-in-law on Jarlath Street. They were of Germanic descent, and I always referred to them as Frau and Herr Tuschak. I looked around as I was leaving their residence at this beautiful street, and lo and behold out came a friend and colleague of mine at our hospital. In speaking with him for a few moments, I looked across the street and saw that there was a home for sale. I told Donna about this, and we checked it out. Without a doubt, this was to be our home, and it became so in short fashion. It was not a block away from Phillip Rogers School, and its principal was a Dr. Benjamin Elkin, both educator and author. A few of his published works of note were The 6 Foolish Fishermen and Lucky and the Giant. His 1957 book, *Gillespie and the Guards*, was a Caldecott Honor Book.

We moved to Jarlath Street in 1965. Donna and I were thirty-one years old. What a lucky find for us and such a joy that it would literally take hundreds of pages to reflect on our good fortune. Our parents fell in love with the home and our intent to remain in the city. You remember how I worshiped my dad. He was not rich in fame or fortune, but how he gave of himself over and over again is reflected in this purchase. My father immediately, without question, gave us fifteen thousand dollars as a down payment on this beautiful home, which in those days cost fifty thousand dollars. Being of low income, I could not pay them back immediately but did so in another way many years later. I remember both families pitching in, carrying out old rugs and cleaning out closets and cabinets as only families would do in those good old days.

The house was a Georgian with a two-car garage. It was built on an angle with a larger-than-standard lot. Our living room was spacious and looked out on a jalousie porch, consisting of multiple slats of glass operated by a crank; jalousie (louvered) windows were a common sight along porches in the 1950s and '60s. In later years, we converted this to a large den that could be used all year round. The dining room had doors that led to that porch/den. We had a smaller den on the first floor, a nice sized kitchen, and a beautiful curved staircase that led to four bedrooms upstairs.

Jarlath Street, that great street, was teaming with children matching our kids' ages, and basically, they never had to leave the street to enjoy themselves with their newfound friends. Many of the parents close to our age immediately became our friends and to this day are still friends.

Our next-door neighbors and best friends had a German shepherd dog. One day, the dog somehow got loose, leaving its yard. All the neighbors cowered, and so did this poor dog. He was away from his home with nothing to guard. His usual threatening bark was gone, and his head was hanging low. Along comes my wife, who gently took the dog by his collar and led him back to his yard. What was her reward? As soon as the dog was back in his domain, he rewarded Donna with a bark and a snarl.

There was a beautiful park just a block east and just South of Phillip Rogers School. There were outdoor tennis courts. But most of all, during the summer, we would all gather outside to enjoy each other's company. And in the winter, oh some of those winters, there was my love Donna shoveling out walkways. Ah she loved the peace and quiet of a snowy night. And there was always helping the neighbors shovel their cars out. I think she was trying to protect me with my asthma.

Donna and I loved flowers, and we had annuals, perennials, fruit trees, vegetables, you name it. For years, we did all our own gardening. I even converted the backyard grass into a patio.

We had a few nursing homes in our neighborhood just a few blocks from our home. Every few days, the flowers in front of our house would disappear. I assumed that animals were to blame. However, one day as

I walked out of my garage door, I saw a kindly old lady speaking to herself about her beautiful garden and the need to take them home to her mate. She imagined this to be her own home. I gently walked her back, as I recall, to the nursing home. We had incidences where people would leave the home, get lost, and in some instances, never return. This was my first realization of the danger associated with dementia.

After a few years, we decided to build a waterfall at the end of our yard. It was indeed a beautiful thing to see. One year, we decided to have some fish live in our water ponds and enjoy our outdoor paradise. It turned out to be paradise or fish heaven for some little critters. We went down to the lakefront and a fishing hut to buy some fish usually used as bait for larger fish—in our case minnows. We rushed home, made sure the pumps were operative, and tossed these critters in. We watched them and welcomed them into their new home, but alas and alack, within sixty seconds, they all belly-upped. Oops, I'd forgotten our pool was chlorinated. I was a mass murderer.

As summer faded to fall, we prepared for Chicago's winters. There was a funny tradition in Chicago and perhaps in other urban areas. People would cart out chairs or anything they could find to save their parking space during the snowy winters, and boy did we experience some. The Blizzard of '67 proved the wisdom behind the Chicago saying, "If you don't like the weather, just wait a minute." Only two days before, the temperature had reached a record 65 degrees. The Chicago Blizzard of 1967 struck on January 26, 1967, with a record-setting 23 inches (58 cm) of snow falling on Chicago and its suburbs before the storm abated the next morning. To this day, it is the worst blizzard in Chicago history. The snow fell continuously on Chicago from 5:02 a.m. on Thursday, January 26, until 10:10 a.m. Friday when twenty-three inches had fallen. The storm played havoc with commuters, stranding thousands of people and leaving an estimated eight hundred busses and fifty thousand automobiles abandoned on the city streets and expressways. On the Thursday, I was working in a satellite office on Peterson Avenue. I literally just made it into our driveway. They say lots of people were stranded far away from their homes and often at their place of work. Those who could do so found some lodging with friends or in a nearby hotel. It is said that nine months later, there was a large number of babies born.

Our home became the headquarters central for the next few days, and the men reverted to becoming hunters once more. We would look for any trucks carrying the necessary supplies for young families. We were able to stop several of these and purchased as much milk and bread as we could. We all hunkered down in our basement, with its fireplace. Several nurses from a local hospital had also joined us. You can say we were the first survivalists, before that became a popular television show.

In mid-January 1979, piled up on top of snow already on the ground, there was another blizzard, producing a record accumulation of twenty-nine inches. January and February were Chicago's notoriously snowy months, and there was nothing we could do about it.

Winter snows in turn make us long for the sun.

I recently I saw the movie, *A Raisin in the Sun* on the Turner Classic Movie channel. It reminded me that Donna and I saw this play's debut in Chicago. Lorraine Hansberry's *A Raisin in the Sun* is surely the greatest Chicago play, and we were privileged to see it. The story, which is current to me, having seen it recently, goes like this: When the Younger family receives a ten-thousand-dollar life insurance check, the promise of a better life seems to be just around the corner. But the family struggles with conflicting ideas about how to use the money (boy, how this strikes home for me) by investing it in a harebrained scheme or their plans to buy a home in the white Clybourne Park neighborhood with its racist intolerance. Set just before the civil rights and women's movements, this powerful and beloved play celebrates faith, courage, and the human spirit while also casting a spotlight on issues that still plague Chicago many years after its premiere. Who was it who said, "Why can't we all just get along?"

The reason that this strikes home for me today is that I had a son for whom money was the center of life and other children with other ideas, some of which I understand much better today and some that still defy my understanding.

Yes, those were good times. Neighbors popped in on neighbors through front doors, back doors, it did not matter. And there were ample friends to dine with, go to movies with, and play all sorts of games with. Yuck, bridge—Donna and I had to analyze everything we did wrong, as we usually lost. We hit upon the solution of cross teaming, Donna with someone else and I with another. Who could argue? It could be part of another book *The Many Ways to Keep Your Marriage Going Strong.*

These early days on Jarlath Street were some of the best years of our life. Though we have gone from our home, it still remains our home in my daily thoughts and dreams. We returned several times for the annual Jarlath Street block party, mainly to visit our old friends as well as the street we loved. Donna referred to these early days as the first quarter of her life.

Donna made many close friends in our neighborhood. Barbara told me Donna was the first neighbor she met. Our back door and Barbara and Marty's front door were next to each other. Donna was a night owl, so Barbara would often see her kitchen light burning as she would be passing the night baking, reading, or indulging in her beloved late-night treat, ice cream. Barbara remembers sneaking out of her door as her family slept and joining Donna for a cup of coffee. They would spend the night talking, laughing, and solving the problems of the world. These would become their favorite memories of time spent together. Barbara learned to bake, swapped recipes, and tried new hairstyles or the latest needlepoint stitch.

I must talk about her artistic manner and other forms of creativity. Much of this is reflected in her needlepoint works, which many feel are magnificent works of art. She especially liked to create and capture the faces of beautiful women. I love to look at her needlepoints and her artistry with admiration.

Barbara and Marty had a son, Reid, with medical concerns. He was in and out of the hospital for two years and had numerous surgeries. We helped them on occasion, and Donna was often at their house holding Reid, caring for his needs, so that Barbara had time for other obligations.

Barbara told me that Donna was the envy of the neighborhood. Her baking was legendary, and an invitation to one of Donna's parties was coveted. She told me that you always felt special being with Donna.

She was a marvelous cook, and I was proud of her presentation and preparation of the food, be it for our little family or our friends. She won first prize in many cooking contests during that period of our life. What

I'm most proud of was her recognition by Bev Bennett, a food critic for the *Chicago Sun-Times*. She made the newspaper, and to this day, I have a framed picture of her smiling and holding her unique delicacy. She called it a Scandinavian pinwheel. I can't describe how it was made, but her family and friends can tell you how it tasted. For many years, she used this as an appetizer, and in later years, I enjoyed helping her put it together. She was very gracious in passing the recipe on to her friends.

Another friend talked to me about those years as well. Her name was Irene. Irene called Donna the maven of Jarlath Street. The word *maven* comes from a Hebrew word that denotes understanding or wisdom in general.

Irene told me she thought Donna was the best cook, seamstress, and hostess and the ultimate interior decorator. "Who let me dress up in costume clothes? Donna did!" she said. "We'd go shopping together, lunched together, and gossiped together."

Irene remembered that we had a block party. At the last one, they nominated Donna as Queen of Jarlath Street. With a Burger King crown as her tiara and a new broom as her scepter, Bella Donna joined her subjects in a regal march down the street.

Donna, Irene, and Barbara were there for each other in good times and bad. During Donna's dark days, she cried and they listened; during Barbara's or Irene's dark days, they cried and she listened.

Barbara remembers that Donna did not offer judgment—opinions yes, prejudice no—and she was someone Barbara trusted. She was honest about her life and who she was. "There were no airs," Barbara told me. "The children were children, not royalty, our husbands not gods."

Both Barbara and Irene expressed that they miss Donna. "We were sad when disappointed or were joyous with each other when a light did shine above. If that is not love and friendship, I'm not sure what is. I talk to her often. I know she can hear me and know that I love her always. At the end of each call or visit, we always said, 'I love you,'" Barbara told me.

"I truly miss the comfort of knowing when I looked across the street … she was there. She was my very special friend—honest, loyal, funny, and giving—and will live forever in my heart," Irene said.

This poignant expression from these dear friends creates a melancholy feeling but also a warm one knowing that Donna, my dear Donna, was loved by many.

I have to acknowledge these true friends who are as caring of this widower. To this day, I still see dear Barbara and Irene and their families and think of my dear, dear friend Jerry, who passed on but never from my heart.

I also acknowledge all the other neighbors who played a role in Donna's life, making our time on Jarlath Street so wonderful.

Chapter 15

● ●

Smiling and Sailing through It All

"Side by Side" is a popular song with lyrics by Gus Kahn and music by Harry M. Woods. It was sung by many artists but is probably best known in a 1953 recording by Kay Starr.

> Oh we ain't got a barrel of money.
> Maybe we're ragged and funny.
> But we'll travel along singin' a song.
> Side by side …

Yes, just as long as we were together, as the song says, we shared it all. You see, I was a workaholic. I loved my profession and didn't think of getting away from it all. I had settled into my professional life full-time and with much zeal. I enjoyed the challenges of medicine but more so the chance to help people. I worked many long hours making hospital calls, office calls, and some house calls. Donna, in her own way, was the center of our life, keeping the home fires burning. Her job was a twenty-four/seven one. This is not a mundane task. Let no one think that a stay-at-home parent is not a full-time job. She had so many talents and a tolerance for my being away so much. She was used to it, as her dad was a physician.

Donna felt that we had to get away from it from time to time, seeking diversion and more time together. Among her many talents was the ability to save some money and always arrange our getaways, and one of our favorite modes of travel was the cruise.

As I promised you some humor amid the sentimentality, this next section will not be a travelogue or a boast about all the places we saw and all the people we met. It was literally planes, trains, automobiles, buses, and most of all, cruising. Aside from the trips with parents and children, we had various traveling partners, many of them with interesting quirks and many trips with peculiar events. These are some I would like to focus on.

Our very first cruise was one I shall never forget. There was a couple we were traveling with. Donna and I were invited to sit at the chief purser's table, and so we did—that is, Donna and I did. That couple vanished at dinnertime, and we never knew why. The food was exquisite, classically served so that could not be the reason. I hope it wasn't us. To this day, however, it remains a mystery. My pal brought his violin along on this trip, and we could hear him scratching away earnestly. One can think of it as the phantom of the cruise ship. Every time we reached a port of call, one could see or hear my friend fiddling away. When we were at sea, we noticed several people missing every few days. In retrospect, these were elderly folks who passed away. One could notice the coffins being removed from the ship early in the dawn. This brings me to the most interesting part of that cruise. Our fiddling friend was also interested in exotic birds.

Trinidad and Tobago has a national bird, both the white and scarlet ibis. Our friend decided we had to see these exotic birds and especially when they returned to their nests, white back to their nest, scarlet to theirs. Hum, is there prejudice even in the animal kingdom or is this something inborn? I certainly hope the latter. They have probably done the same thing generation after generation, either intuitively or by genetic programming. In those days, security was not a big problem and so my dear friend arranged this tour. It would begin in a small boat and end when the birds returned to their nests. This was usually at sunset. One has to realize that most ships leave port close to this time. They usually bellow out the warning three times. By the second sound, I panicked (as usual) and had to pay off the boatmaster and the other guests to allow us to reach shore and scurry back to the cruise ship. Somehow, we made it back, or I would be writing this near some palm trees and far, far away.

One of our other cruises brought us to the eastern side, the Atlantic side of Panama. We were then set free to travel to Balboa on the Pacific side. As I mentioned earlier, security was not an issue in those days when leaving a cruise ship as it is today (except in this case, problems stemming from drugs, el presidente, and revolutions) … We commissioned a taxi driver to take us on this pleasant trip and negotiated a reasonable fee. As we approached Panama City, one could hear the tumultuous sounds of a revolution taking place. At this point, it was not I or Donna who panicked but our driver. This may have been a ploy for more money, as he grandly stated that he had to rush home to protect his family. He started to open the doors and leave us at the roadside. You know the old song rum and Coca-Cola, etc., and working for the Yankee dollar? He sure was! With the greenbacks transferred from my pocket to his, he grandly turned around, forgot his family for the moment, and took us back to the place where we had started. It was many years before we actually saw the Panama Canal and the wondrous locks.

Another time, we traveled to French Polynesia. We were inspired by Paul Gauguin. I'm sure that most of you know about Gauguin and French Polynesia. Paul Gauguin (1848–1903) is one of the true larger-than-life figures in art history. The key feature in his makeup is his constant yearning for an exotic paradise. He sought it in the bohemian arts community at Pont-Aven on the coast of Brittany and later on the South Seas island of Tahiti and an Island of the Kings called Morrea. Morrea is Polynesia's second most popular tourist attraction after Tahiti. Located a mere twelve miles (nineteen kilometers) west of the island of Tahiti, Morrea is a triangular island encircled by a lagoon of translucent green, fringed by an azure-blue Polynesian sea. Covering an area of fifty-one square miles, it is the only other major island in the Windward group of the Society Islands besides Tahiti.

This was to be our most exotic trip traveling south of the equator on to Tahiti. We flew to Hawaii where we were to meet our cruise ship. We were most excited, and I most of all to see the beautiful ladies of Polynesia promised me by the impressionistic work of Gaugain.

We reached Morrea, and indeed, it was a beautiful sight to see, a virtual paradise. From a distance, Donna spied a circle of women creating flowery crowns for one's head. They were all busy, heads down, with fingers twirling. The flowers were beautiful, and Donna influenced me to go into this little bit of Polynesian paradise. I gleefully did so. I was very disappointed as I got closer. "My, oh my," said I under my breath. The women were not exactly young lasses but late middle-aged, rather stout and lacking their good features of days gone by. Donna, that gracious soul, compelled me to accept their flowery crown and to sit with them for a bit. I'm sure she only wanted to capture this on film.

This whole incident reminded me of another song sung by Bob Dylan, "Where Have All the Flowers Gone." I was thinking, *Where have all the maidens gone?* Bob would say, "Gone to soldiers every one." I was thinking that there were no young maidens on this island, as they all left for other places, such as Hawaii, or maybe even a chance to become an authentic Dorothy Lamour–type in Hollywood. Ah well, the day was not wasted, as we dined elegantly on some bread and cheese sitting by the shore.

On another cruise, we ran into a bad storm at sea and waves that were forty feet high, if not higher. Donna was seasick and in our tiny cabin. My friend Don and I were not seasick, and I bravely walked to the front of the ship (inside of course!). I returned from time to time to check on Donna and urge her to get out of bed and go to some common area.

When we reached the front of the ship, we spied three gentlemen and a few decks of cards. Don liked to gamble, and at times, I had a similar itch. One guy had a cowboy hat on, and I made up my mind that he was a professional gambler. And so we sat down and introduced ourselves to the three men. I was told they were playing a game called Middle Eastern poker. The California guy had a regular name, like Jim or John. The other two guys had names compatible with the game that they had chosen to play. After a reasonable period of time, I asked for their countries of origin. Are you ready for this? One fellow was from Iraq and the other from Israel. You know, if I had a political bent, I could've forged a peace pact long before many of our presidents gave it a shot, as they are still trying to do today. Goodness gracious, I could've been invited to Oslo to receive my peace prize. Both the opportunity and the poker game were lost to me. I walked away a loser but ultimately a winner as Donna recovered nicely.

In addition to the cruises, Donna and I took a few bus tours, one to Western Canada and the other Nova Scotia. First off, we'll start with the western tour. We toured the western United States and Canada, staying in many interesting places. Yellowstone National Park was extremely interesting although one could not set one's watch relying on Old Faithful. We were so happy holding hands, seeing sights we had never seen before, and I loved her ability to be so extroverted. I was the quiet one and usually held back. On the other hand, she made many friends, and we actually reunited with some of them years later. As our last destination, we visited Banff National Park, Lake Louise, Canada. The tour was beautiful, and we were staying in a place that looked like a castle. Donna was very pleased with this trip.

On the last night before heading home, our group had a final dinner party, and we were through at an early hour. Nobody seemed tired or ready to leave. Donna saw a piano in the main area. With that beautiful smile of hers, she said that her husband was a marvelous pianist and would be glad to entertain our little group. Of course, I could not refuse, and about thirty people gathered around the piano as I went from song to song without the need for any sheets of music. I could always play by ear. After an hour or so, I turned away from the piano and looked behind me. Lo and behold, there must've been a hundred people or more listening to the concert and applauding when I was through. They must've thought that I was the entertainment for that night. Well, I guess I was!

The trip to Nova Scotia was very significant for me. Of course, the seafood was great. Our tours of the fishing villages and walking to the tip of the continent to watch Atlantic whales at play were great moments. I also remember an uncanny moment when we toured and walked into an old cabin. At home, Donna and I had started a new discussion group with our friends so that we could discuss various problems in honesty. We called the group EMES, the Ashkenazi term for the truth. There carved into this old wooden table in the cabin of Nova Scotia were four letters, *EMES*. To me, this was uncanny, and we took it as an omen that the group would be successful.

The finest moment for us, though, was when we got to Halifax Bay, Nova Scotia, a point of entry for many refugees and immigrants. Donna knew that this was the very same place that my grandparents had entered into the New World and ultimately brought us together. Grandfather, a very serious man, always had a special affinity with my wife, and my grandmother adored her. That, my friends, was our biggest thrill.

Our trips together were wonderful, but fellow travelers joined us on these trips, be they by land or sea. They were Harold (who has passed on) and Eleanor (still a friend), Norma and Howard, Howard and Harriet (who are both in a better place, I know), our buddies Carol and Vern, and Dianne and Don (rest in peace, my friend).

Smile" is a pop song, which originally appeared in the movie *Modern Times*. Charlie Chaplin wrote the music to "Smile" for the movie. Moreover, Chaplin composed the music to many of his films and was an accomplished piano player with a knack for being creative. The lyrics were added later by John Turner and Geoffrey Parsons. The song has been covered by the elite of the musical world—Nat King Cole, Tony Bennett, Michael Bublé, Josh Groban, Justin Bieber, Eric

Clapton, Janelle Monae, and Michael Jackson. The following are lyrics from that song:

> Smile, though your heart is aching
> Smile, even though it's breaking
> When there are clouds in the sky
> you'll get by ...

My dear wife had a beautiful smile, spontaneous and oh so real. As I look around the house at every picture of her, there she is smiling at me. Oh, there were times when she scowled at something or someone (usually me). She had a lot to smile about in the early days that she sometimes called the first quarter of her life. I will define these quarters later on and speak for Donna in her own words that were written down. She loved her home, her family, and her friends and loved to be creative and entertaining in the most elegant manner.

When we weren't traveling, we also spent a lot of time with her hobbies and in those days did a lot of antique hunting and paperweight collecting. My own personal hobby was to find old walking sticks or canes. She was president of her ladies' group and organized many events. I must admit to a separation anxiety when she left for the evening. I couldn't help it, but if she was away for a period of time, there I was gazing through a window, just as I did with my mom years earlier. I did exactly the same thing with my kids as they became more independent.

Yes, there were stormy times ahead, but not in those early days. This part of my life was more important to me than anything else. We were partners in life, and the times I spent with her were joyous. The pride within me was enormous. I felt very lucky to have her as my life partner.

Chapter 16

. . . .

Travailing on Together

Our Smiles Fade along Life's Travels

> There are smiles that make us happy,
> there are smiles that make us blue,
> There are smiles that have a tender meaning
> That the eyes of love alone may see ...
> —"Smiles," words and music by J. Will Callahan and Lee
> S. Roberts (1927), recorded by Benny Goodman (1936)

This brings me to a difficult point in our memoir and our dance of life. That first part of our life was blessed with parents, our togetherness, our kids, our friends, our activities, and our naïveté. The dance of our life became frantic, hectic, and trying. We were doing our thing, our children were doing theirs, and the surviving grandparents had their own agenda. We had parties and confirmations for our three children and still enjoyed life to the fullest. Then, based on many things, mostly centered on the loss of family members, life for us changed forever.

Donna had already lost her mother to breast cancer at an early age, as I mentioned. Donna was in her late twenties when her mother died. The 1970s brought on further sadness. In 1975, my father succumbed to an illness, which was prolonged and extremely stressful. Donna and I were forty-one years old at that time. Up to that point, Dad was a great help to Donna with various tasks. They had a great relationship. He had developed pneumonia, and on the day he was to go home from the hospital, he was sitting in the radiology department when he collapsed with a heart attack. He was rushed back to intensive care, where he lingered for many days. He developed a heart aneurysm and a dangerous rhythm to his heartbeat. It was called ventricular fibrillation. My mother and I watched them apply the defibrillator pads almost on a daily basis. Here is the sad part. Having stayed in the hospital each day, I decided to take a few hours off to play my beloved game of tennis. That was the first time I had left the hospital during the daytime vigil. At night, I would usually see my mom home and then return to my own home. On that day, she remained at the hospital. I was to pick her up later on. Unfortunately, a severe storm erupted, and I could not make it back to the hospital as snow began to pile up.

You remember my speaking of premonitions, as I have had them before. On my way home that day, everything turned black in front of my eyes. I shouted out to myself that my father had died at that very moment. I marked the time on the way home, and when I arrived, there was my family waiting for me. I walked in saying that I knew and asked what time he died. It was precisely that moment of bleak darkness I experienced while I was in my car. This then was yet another premonition in my life. There are two more to follow, and they will be related later on ... Anyhow, my mother was marooned at the hospital, but I will never forget the good Sister D., who gave her shelter and comfort until I could pick her up.

When it was the day of the funeral for my dad, the snow was still piled quite high, and we literally had to dig our way to his gravesite.

One year after that, Aunt Lillian (Minnie) succumbed to ovarian cancer. I had referred her to MD Anderson Cancer Center, and her devoted husband, Uncle Adolph, gave up everything to be with her.

My father-in-law followed a few years later. While showering, he discovered a huge mass in his abdomen. He came to see me when I found that his spleen was markedly enlarged. The diagnosis of chronic myelogenous leukemia soon followed. Together with a colleague of mine, we did everything we could, but he also succumbed to a dreadful illness.

One year later, I lost my dear cousin Charlene, a quiet and noble girl. She developed a bizarre form of lung cancer that was actually rapidly enlarging to her chest wall. It is my feeling that as a teacher, she had to work in the expansion Quonset huts, which were built speedily and filled with asbestos fibers. She was also exposed to secondhand smoke.

Other uncles and aunts on both sides of the family died during the difficult seventies, as I called them. You remember that Donna's family had the genetic predisposition to cancer, and all of her family succumbed.

Aside from these deaths, there was "trouble in River City," if you remember the play *Seventy-Six Trombones*. We were faced with the drug issues of that era. "Oh no," Donna said. "Oh no," Joel said. "Not our children!"

I promised not to delve into specifics, and I shall not do so. It is always self-obligation and self-honesty for those we love. I remain a protective and sheltering father.

In essence, I had to find a way to express myself and turned to my dad's ability to put things down in writing. Some call it journaling; others, including me, call it a release valve. At this point in my life, I was generally a silent man who in social and professional life did a lot of listening. I was also engaged in self-doubt and self-blame, and having inherited my dad's abilities in the written word, it all burst out of me onto paper.

I ask that you indulge me, as I was also engaged in this dance of life, and in part it is a shared memoir, albeit a dedication to Donna. For those of you who are musicians, our dance had become a fugue, but I am thankful it was never a pavane.

I always was concerned that adoption played a role in our family dynamic. So I spoiled them, always trying to be a super dad. This is reflected in some of the anguish and expressions that follow. I became rather creative at that time and, yes, during a period of depression wrote a lot of this. Donna was struggling as well. I think her way at that time made her the stronger parent. We were both emotionally in stress, but she always handled things directly. You can see though that my doubts and fears led to a method of my own. I continued with denial and depression but found a way to express myself on paper. It was my way.

My Way

In quiet moments of my life,
I sit and ponder of my past.
Those ancient memories, how they last
And hold me captive in review
of older days when life was new,
Of older days with problems few.
When children hovered at my knees
Like hungry chicks with open beaks
To nurture and be cared upon,
Their needs seemed pure when we were young.

But I had time; it gave me joy
To nourish each in their own way.
I gave but did receive in pay
that sweet word *father* rings out clear.
It's what I wanted most to hear.
And know how much they needed me.
And hope that I would satisfy
and trust I'd answer every cry.

God chose these children for our life.
Each one at birth I do recall
The love they brought; it made me whole.
The tenderness, it freed my soul.
My needs were there when I was young.

It's been my doubt; it's been my fear.
This nemesis has been my foe;

I felt inferior. So you see,
That fear completely captured me.

The anxious thoughts they did appear.
The anxious thoughts did bring me fear.
My mind did think they would reject.
Our parenthood they would suspect.

Adopted when they first were born
To me seemed harsh; it seemed a thorn.
A surrogate, that was my fear,
And so I held my children near.

This need was there when they were young,

And so I proved beyond my means.
To jump and run and steer their bikes,
To love and play and read them tales
Of nursery rhymes and Dr. Seuss,
of fantasy and make-believe.
Those tasks of love they did relieve.

My anxious needs to prove to me
That I could meet my destiny.
That I was meant to be their dad,
The only one they'll ever have.

I played this role when I was young,

And as they grew, I let them free,
In my own way, with leniency.
But kept them tied to my own needs,
Tied by my neurotic knot.
To prove to them as well as me,
The best of dads I'd surely be.

I laid my claims to be the best
And rise to duty, rise to test.
To be beyond the common lot.
To give them all beyond extreme.

Ascending to this pedestal,
I know the role; I played it well.
My greatest need to give my all.
My greatest need to give my soul.

That was my need, when they were young

But now, just now, it's called today.
I live with fear; I live with doubt
About the world and all its woe,
About the role I have to play.
Not play! But live it every day.

And so I live with manner tense.
It seems there is no recompense.
Those things I did just yesterday
Are distant dreams lost in today.

Demonic forces are about
To test the mettle of the best.
This evil world won't let me rest,
For as that father of the past,
I still do grieve; my fears they last.

It's still my need, though I'm not young;

As children grow, the problems grow.
And proper choices must be made.
And proper pathways must be laid.
Oh, how we struggle in this world
With that which demons have unfurled,
With crime and anger, sin and woe.
The sons of Hades cast their blow

Upon us all, and there's no rest.
Upon us all, our souls to test.
Demonic forces can't be beat
By bluster, boldness, or conceit;

By giving in or backing out.
Denying all or casting doubt,
Our children hide with different schemes.
They hide while filling pipes of dreams
Or hide within a deadly shroud
Of nuclear threat and chemical cloud.

It seems a shame; they are so young.

We all must work to find a way.
And give up fears and give up fright.
The past is gone and can't return.
The past is gone; it's now today.
Forget the bits of yesterday.

This simple truth is in my soul,
where God and angels do abide.
I need not stand alone and fight
but keep a clear goal in sight

To live a life of hope and cheer,
To try and keep my purpose clear,
To do for others in a way
That lets them grow from day to day.

I'll try to be and not to do.
I'll try to love in ways so new.
And so my final thought is sung
With no more thoughts when I was young.

I continued to struggle. I would call this a period of depression. Hurting as I did, the next poem reflects my struggle in an anecdotal way. Donna was equally disturbed. I can't speak for her, but I know she was right there with me struggling and just trying to cope. I could easily say we were both in a state of deep gloom.

The Struggle

As I sit near the banks of gloom,
As those in ancient Babylon,
The river rears its angry glow,
The currents, deep in anguish flow.
You almost hear it cry and weep.
Perhaps it is my tortured mind.
"What ails thee?" does the river speak.
"What can we do for the Son of Man?
What simple song or sound or rhyme
Can grant you solace at this time?"
"Ah," said I, "there's naught to do.
If I were as a blade of grass
Beneath clouds of blue and sky serene,
I'd soon be crushed by mighty weight."
That brings me to a horrid fate,
And sky turned gray, to bring forth rain,
A tempest that will bring me pain.
Alas, thus spoke my troubled mind.

"Oh no," the grass and clouds do speak.
"You have no power, don't you see?
Although today we seem serene,
Upon this given day we live.
Upon this day real pleasure give,
Yet we too wither and turn gray.
This cycle flows for every kind,
Just as the cycle of your mind.
But not because of plans conceived;

But nature's turns and Godly fate.
Both sorrow and pleasure can update.
So Son of Man, lift up your eyes
And breathe the air that life decrees.
Enjoy the pleasures you can't see;
Enjoy the gift of humankind."
The river of gloom does remind,

Yet still I sit beneath my gloom,
Weaving grief from fabric doom.
I searched in vain for a lady hope,
To find the balm from her own loom.

Oh heavens, source from which we stem,
My spirit crushed beyond the mend.
I cannot bargain or beseech,
and so within my mind I reach.
The river bank of gloom I find,
To look for reason, nothing more.
The earthly bounty I have shared.
Of life's full challenge I had dared.
It's not for me the gloom pervades.
My very soul this gloom invades.

Man's gift to man, our skies are gray.
And to the river I do say
these morbid gifts to bring forth rain.
As white as snow or dread cocaine,
and yes, the earthborn weed I fear
for my own children I hold so dear.

These morbid gifts destroy the mind
and put our sons in troubled way
And hold daughters in their sway.
I weep for them, not me alone.
But sorrow that this world has known,
sorrow deep within my mind.
Man's gift can be a sweet repast.
But some are born of devil's cast
And some bring forth evil spell
That leads to torment, earthly hell
And flow of gloom within the mind.

The river of gloom in murmur low
Reminds me of an endless path.
It flows today from yesterday
and onward to its future path.
So like the circles of my mind
The river was, it is, will be.
Man's thoughts are similar, you see.
If I succumb and join its flow,
Upon it caste all fears to go.
This thought resounds within my mind.

Get up and rise and leave this bank
Of gloom and ever present grief.
This thought indeed does bring relief.
I take my leave; I want no more.
To be depressed at trouble's shore
Again, I search within my mind.

"Come here." I hear this quiet voice.
"Come here within thy very soul
To see the light and spark of hope.
No more to search, no more to grope;
it's in yourself some peace to find.
Within the love you carry deep
Can fear and trouble put to sleep.
Take heart, gain strength, lift up your head.
A kinder shore is straight ahead.
Remember you can do no more.
Moral lessons you have taught;
For others, kinder paths you sought.
By action and by honest deed,
The ones you love may well succeed
And free the gloom within your mind."

Thus, if upon the banks I stay,
With furrowed brow and darkness cast,
I would remain within the past,
and so I leave to find my way
away from gloom. I must now stray
And not be lost there in my mind.

And so my soul did me remind:
"Within yourself there lies a spark,
a part of God that there resides.
It cares for us and path provides
A gift of life, we often find.
That demons cannot tear away.
That evil cannot block the way.

The cosmic embers in our care,
The light from which we often share,
It's there within for us to find.
Patience, listen, it does remind.
If but I heed it will revive.
If but I seek it can survive
And drown the sorrows of my mind.

This epic struggle of my being,
A mighty battle do I wage
to lose all anger and all rage.
I know well what my mind reveals
and what my ego can't conceal.
The truth is never hard to find.
The banks of gloom I now can see
Are mighty struggles in my life.
The mighty struggles to control
The destiny of my own soul.
And so I thank that blade of grass.
The sky of blue and clouds serene
That gently live their destiny,
That gave of truths for me to see,
That gave the wisdom I'd never find.
If banks of gloom invade my mind,
So like the river I will flow
And never seek to find control.
And never think of yesterday,
And on to peace within my mind.

You can see I was using the metaphoric method, trying to get out of my depression. I think this period was as hard for Donna, and it did affect our relationship somewhat. At this point, I would come home from work, stay within myself, and go to bed early. I lost a lot of weight from a bodily standpoint but carried a great deal of emotional weight. Donna, however, started to stay up to all hours doing her needlepoint work while watching her favorite TV shows. I can still remember her distinctive laugh as she listened to Johnny Carson (or whomever) on the *Tonight Show*. She also loved all of the awards shows and would call her girlfriends up during the show to gossip about the stars, the award winners, and the styles of the day. That was her way of coping.

In the next poem, you can see us trying so hard to recover. Journaling through poetry was helpful for me and often was the antidote for my melancholy. Donna too had many moments of sadness but had her own release valve with her special friends. We were not always open with the situations at hand, and each of us had our own way of coping. At the same time, we were looking to find a form of support that would unify us, so we didn't have to struggle individually. Some friends did not always understand what she was going through and often made things worse by offering their advice. We needed some special help for our struggles. Thank goodness, we had each other and this did not break us apart, for our bond as in our wedding vows was for better or worse.

As we were searching, I kept up with my journaling and imagery, looking for a new road or pathway for us to travel together.

The Path to Peace

To slumber near still waters,
to live and not just cope.
To leave the lane of said despair
and find the street of hope.

To search for a Valley of sweet content,
To rest my head in peace.
To find the road to happy thoughts,
So spiritual pain may cease.

I keep within my restless mind
Those pathways of despair.
And so I find the pitfalls
Of the Devil's trap and lair.

You ask me why I'm on this route.
My answer is I care.
To chase my fears and chase my fright
For loved ones in despair.

I rushed to points of personal pain,
To share their deepest plight.
I know this route will bring me naught;
It's something I can't fight.

And so I choose to end this run
Along a worthless way

And try to find the path of peace
So pain can go away.

You can see how troubled I was in those days with my bouts of recurrent depression, but this form of journaling through poetry was helpful for me and often was the antidote for my melancholy. During these times, my poetic nature burst forth. Donna too had many moments of sadness but as a release valve had her friends to speak with. I was looking for other means of support for her as well.

My younger son, Ken, and daughter, Cheryl, today often tell me to let the past go. They have to understand that it was about us and our own survival.

Chapter 17

• •

The New Road to Travel

Families Anonymous (or Friends Always)

In 1978, we were forty-four years old. We had not yet found the road that we both could travel on emotionally and spiritually. So I continued after my workday was over to sit down and express those thoughts yet lingering in my mind. Donna was more practical about finding a solution that was more concrete than my poetic yearnings.

Thought of Another Time and Place
The Circles of My Mind

Again, again, the wheels are spinning.
Spinning on to cast my fate.
And my anxious mind arriving
Once again at horror's gate.

Weaving, churning, ever turning,
Giving help without a doubt.

Give no thought to false direction
And what true help is all about.

Weaving, turning, ever circling,
How my head begins to spin.
Soon the past begins to tighten,
Trapping morbid thoughts within.

Fear has gripped my very fiber.
Flames of guilt surround my soul.
Pangs of pain encircle reason
As I spin on to find my role.

Spinning, spinning, mind in motion
In a never changing mode.
At best, it's time to change direction
And to try a different road.

Move on, move on, and change the pattern.
Just maintain a firm resolve
To retain those things that matter,
Keeping hope lest it dissolve.

Once again, the wheels are spinning
In the circles of my mind.
To arrive in proper motion
On the road of humankind.

Spinning, spinning, ever moving.
All of us are in the flow

To a future destination
As we let our old ways go.

That road did arrive. It was one we had not traveled before. We both came from families where you kept things inside and within the family circle. We needed a place to share our thoughts and emotions together and found it in a self-help group called Families Anonymous. We heard about this group through counselors and social workers, and at that time, it was highly recommended. I often wonder if that group survived. This was a twelve-step program modeled after the original Alcoholic Anonymous. We were not addicted but were the victims of other loved ones' struggles. The program was for parents or significant others like us who were frightened of the time we were living in, fearful of the anger welling up around the world, and struggling with our demonic fear of nuclear war and the emergence of the drug era. I was reluctant and fearful of sharing our problems, but my wife assured me that this would be a good solution for us as a married couple.

The danger of drugs has never left my thoughts to this day, as it remains prevalent across the world. I say this as I sometimes wonder why we sent our young people to Afghanistan with its mountains and caves into a war like no other, which these brave young people had to face. Such loss of our blood and treasure. Oil has always been a big issue in the Middle East, but so are the poppy fields and their main product opium, which is a major export in Afghanistan. I am still amazed at the futility of it all and the killing of our children in ways other than the battlefield. You remember the poem that goes, "In Flanders field, the poppies grow amidst the crosses row on row." That, my friends, was sad in an entirely different manner.

"Getting to Know You"
Rodgers and Hammerstein

Getting to know you
Getting to know all about you
Getting to like you
Getting to hope you like me.

"The Serenity Prayer"

God grant me the serenity
To accept the things I cannot change.
To change the things I can.
And the wisdom to know the difference.

Families Anonymous was indeed hard work. We joined the group in 1978. I won't go into detail as to how long we belonged to the group or the fact that Donna, I, and others started several new chapters along the way. Most of these meetings took place in hospitals or churches. We just had to bring our own coffee supplies and of course our honesty, if we were to succeed.

Some of it was very tough to understand. No person really likes defeat or loss of control, and Donna and I initially felt that we could handle each problem by ourselves and continue to manage them away. After many sessions and listening to many people, we understood that there was no gain from the continued pain of denial, anger, or depression. Listening to others with stories so similar was a healing balm and savior of our life during that period.

Donna also volunteered to speak at high schools. Once we were interviewed on a Chicago television station. We were not important. The problem of substance abuse and its effect on young minds was!

There is a special meaning to the choice of "Getting to Know You." Of course, it was getting to know ourselves, new friends, and acquaintances along the way. But this song has special meaning to me in an entirely different manner.

There were many talented people in this organization, and somewhere along the way, we decided to put the program to music. I was the designated pianist and along with Donna and two other ladies, created several different shows. We entertained many church groups and other organizations aligned with the twelve-step program. We were always well received, and this project brought us diversion from daily problems and an accomplishment to be proud of. The merry band traveled from north to south and east to west, and we always had dinner together before the performance. One of the songs was "Getting to Know You," and this was to be our song. Truthfully, in this duet, I could see Donna's beautiful hazel eyes sparkling, while feeling real joy within my heart. It helped us express our love for each other over and over again.

As I promised levity as well as seriousness in this memoir, there is one amusing story that stands out. One night, when I was a leader for that evening, we were interrupted by two men who entered the meeting room. They helped themselves to coffee, nodded hello, and sat down. We were intent on going through the evening's program when the two of them suddenly got up to leave. I can never forget what one man said to the other, and I quote, "Let's get out of here; these guys are drunks." Apparently, they were recovering alcoholics and thought it was an Alcoholics Anonymous meeting. We were not drinkers, just group thinkers looking for the commonality in our collective lives.

I'm proud of Donna's participation in this group. She was an excellent participant in our meetings. She became a mentor to some, always loving and caring for all, and was completely honest. Donna, in spite of her own problems, was there to lend a helping hand to anyone in need and at any moment. There were many in crisis at that time in the 1980s, and she took a personal interest in all of our friends, spending hours on the phone or having a cup of coffee with anyone who called her.

Some folks have not reached her level of understanding and never will. As a result, she participated in a TV program about drugs (on ABC Chicago), asking that her face not be shown in protection of our family's anonymity. She was also invited as a guest speaker at several high schools where they were promoting drug awareness.

During that period, our children were exposed to two threatening clouds. There was a fear of the Cold War turning into an atomic war and at the same time a drug crisis. I refer to these as the nuclear cloud and the drug cloud; both weighed heavily on many families. One night at a meeting, a couple walked in, sat down, and introduced themselves by first names only. I knew the gentleman as a child psychiatrist specializing in drug addiction. And here they were confronted with the same issue. I, of course, kept quiet, protecting his anonymity. As they say, no one is immune. It happens to many and to people in all stations of life.

During this same period of time, my wife had a sudden visual crisis. She could not see out of one eye, and it had turned a milky, cloudy color. She had developed an unusual eye condition of unknown cause. It is called keratoconus. Keratoconus is an eye disease that affects the structure of the cornea. The cornea is the clear tissue covering the front of the eye. The shape of the cornea slowly changes from the normal round shape to a cone shape. The eye bulges out. This causes vision problems and sometimes, as in her case, an actual rupture of the cornea. She went to see a specialist and was told she needed a corneal transplant. The transplant would be available when there was a cornea available. Unfortunately, this had to come from some poor individual who died, usually through a motorcycle or car accident. She had to be ready to enter the hospital within hours' notice when the cornea arrived. The operation was a success; the other eye never gave her any problem, but she always had to wear special lenses made to fit over the unusual shape of her cornea. I watched her put these lenses in with difficulty, and it broke my heart. Nothing, however, stopped her from caring about others and sharing openly and honestly.

Using poetic license, let me relate how we felt with these new friends.

We walked into this special room;
Some people were assembled to weave a loom
Of understanding, compassion, and strength to clasp
A new step, a message so hard to grasp.

Slowly, we emerged from our ivory tower,
Regaining some faith in a higher power,
Learning to live in a meaningful way,
Nurtured by care that was coming our way.

This wonderful program did freely reveal
That a tortured soul could mend and heal.
They call it FA; to our needs it attends,
But we call it hope, and each of you friends.

I want you to hear from a very special friend of Donna's who came into this group but also came into our life. The following is from a letter from Carole (Vern is her husband).

Carol told me that Families Anonymous (when they joined in 1982) was the beginning of a beautiful and very special relationship between our two families. We seemed to bond quickly, and the closeness continued to grow. We went out socially quite often.

She remembers Donna as a wonderful cook and a great baker, famous for her cheesecakes and that special appetizer called a pinwheel, which upon getting the recipe from Donna she prepared for her friends and family.. She remarked that there was also her frosted chocolate chip cookie in a pizza pan, a favorite of her family and friends.

She went on to say that Vern and she were privileged to be invited for barbeques, New Year's Eve (lots of singalongs with me playing the piano along with several games), Passover with their Russian friends, and Sara's early birthday parties. Her granddaughter, Raquela, was a little younger, but they brought her over to visit the teddy bears displayed on the steps. They sure had fun.

She related how we traveled together to New Orleans, St. Louis, Boston, and Nova Scotia (with the birth name of our EMES group carved in a desk). Our trip to the Grand Tetons in 1997 brought back special memories.

Carol told me that she and Donna loved shopping together for clothes and went to a jewelry show, which got her started collecting thimbles.

A favorite memory of hers was calling Donna for every awards show on television. They would stay on the telephone to the end, critiquing the hairdos, the jewelry, and of course the clothes.

Donna was famous for her beautiful needlepoint crafts, and Carol treasured the pillow and the eyeglass case she made for her. She went on to say that the pillow is the first thing she sees in the morning and the last thing she sees at night. Sentimentally, she remarked that it brings back such fond memories and is a great comfort to her.

Her emotional thought in ending was that she missed Donna very much and was grateful for the nearly thirty treasured years she shared with a special friend. I am personally touched by the feelings and love shown to Donna by all her friends.

Chapter 18

Looking for Peace

Somewhere over the rainbow Way up high,
There's a land that I heard of once in a lullaby
If happy little bluebirds fly beyond the rainbow
Why, oh why can't I?
—from "Somewhere over the Rainbow," music by Harold
Arlen and lyrics by E. Y. Harburg

This, of course, is Judy Garland's signature song, but to me, it seems a suitable title for the next part of our dance through life. For those of you not familiar with musical terms, this next period of our life's dance was like a scherzo, a very lively and unpredictable part of classical music.

I relate this to the early times of our life. Some were happy days, and as you shall see, some were not so good. I was so proud of Donna and her talent and elegance through it all. Our relationship with each other was solid without any doubt or fear that we were ever to part.

Our eldest son, Raymond, grew up and grew distant from us. He seemed to be happy and content in his preteen years. I remember when he was thirteen and when he became a man in the tradition of Mosaic law. At his party, I can never forget his coming up to his mom, giving her a kiss, and saying thank you and, "Mom, this is a great party and the best day of my life." I also remember in these early years he was an excellent athlete and the pitcher for his Little League team. We never missed seeing him play. I also recall that he wished to play high school football, which Donna and I did not allow. We were afraid of inferior high school football gear and the nasty injuries that could occur. Well, he did not play football but nonetheless did incur an injury when he twisted his knee while running on Jarlath Street. He had to go through arthroscopic repair.

Our younger son, Ken, had a few mishaps of his own. The worst event happened when he fell and drove his teeth back into his gums. We were quite worried, but fortunately, these teeth magically reappeared after a lot of specialized care. Perhaps for him, the most frustrating accident occurred when he joined a neighborhood hockey league. His mom always drove him to his sporting events. If memory serves me right, she was there and related to me that he was checked into the board, fractured a limb, and was out for the rest of the season. The frustrating part was that his team won the league championship. I also have to mention that Ken was very artistic and created a family crest, which I enjoy looking at to this day. Someday, I hope he finds it when I am gone and enjoys looking at it as much as his mom and I did.

Our daughter, Cheryl, had a few physical problems as she was growing up. She had the need to wear glasses, which she hated, and not to be different from her brothers, she fractured her wrist while at summer camp and suffered a back injury while riding her mom's bike. Again, it was Donna who had to handle the latest crisis. With all of these mishaps, Donna was always the first to know and the first to respond. I was usually in my medical office or at the hospital. She handled each problem calmly and with dignity. In today's terms, she was the first responder.

Donna loved to make costumes for our children on Halloween, and she also loved to sew. Earlier on, I told you that in keeping busy during our military service, she created several articles of clothing, including a woolen red suit. My daughter one year found the suit and a hat that I had bought for Donna in Europe. On one particular Halloween, Cheryl put on the suit and that European-style hat and grabbed one of my collectible canes. To top it off, she purchased the full-faced mask of an old, not very handsome lady. After putting this all together, she walked into the room and surprised us. Somehow, she fully affected the gait of the elderly. When she walked in, it took us several moments to realize that this was our daughter, and at first glance, it was a chilling vision to behold. We recovered and together enjoyed our daughter's talent and acting skills. Incidentally, on that same Halloween, she won first prize at a Lincolnwood costume party contest.

Donna was beginning to show the effects of her arthritis, which seemed to worsen, as I recall, from the 1980s on. We had always loved going to Orchestra Hall, attending the theater, and dancing. All of these had to be modified or stopped completely. I already told you about the visual problems.

For me, there was asthma. I'd had this as a child, but it had disappeared by the time I was well into my fifties. One year, I developed pneumonia, and the asthma started all over again. I had two major attacks but an earlier one was devastating for Donna, more so than myself, as I lost consciousness. The hospital minister told her that I would probably die. How awful it must've been for my wife to hear such news. I remember that our neighbors Barbara and Marty were at her side then, as they always were up to her final illness. What true friends my wife had, a testament to her personality and to her very being.

Change Yourself

Written by Glen Hughes

In this crazy world you must change yourself

In this open road you must change yourself

In this crazy world you must change yourself

Nothing lasts forever

Managed Care

After my last and most severe attack of asthma in 1986 (when I was fifty-four), I was told that exposure to patients and to hospitals could be dangerous to my health. All of you know the dangers of "super bugs" (each hospital has its own favorite) and the resistance of these bugs to the antibiotics in use. We have all been frightened by the flesh-eating bacteria, the *E. coli* strain that can kill you, and of course methicillin-resistant *Staphylococcus aureus* (MRSA). Today, it's Ebola and a mysterious polio-like enterovirus bug affecting young children.

The severe damage to my lungs and my need for massive doses of a steroid medication would not be compatible with medical practice. So what was I to do? I had one year ahead of me where I was at first homebound, gradually becoming more active. I suffered a great deal of panic and anxiety and had to see a psychologist for some time. Donna had to endure a lot with my anxiety and panic attacks relative to this important change in our life. The last days of my own medical practice were in 1986, but I always retained my medical license, thankfully. In that important year, Donna and I were fifty-four years old.

Those years of illness turned out to be a blessing in disguise for both of us. Donna at that time showed her great resilience and faith in our life together. She also had more time to spend with me, and we started to go to the theater and the Chicago Symphony Orchestra concerts, and Donna started to entertain more, as she had her spouse at home. We walked a lot and talked more; it was like a jump start to a new life, as I was divorced from the grueling task of leaving her many an evening to make house calls and rushing back to the hospital. I think this was the time that she accelerated her interest in her needlepoint work. She also had time to be her own person, going out with her friends and doing a lot of charity work for many organizations. Her very favorite charities were St. Jude's Hospital and the Make-a-Wish Foundation, things centered around children. She did all of this as I was figuring out the next steps in our life.

I returned to my music and studied classical music once again. I reached a measure of success to the point where my teacher wanted me to participate in recitals. As they say, though "them days were gone forever," and I bowed out.

The second activity was taking art lessons, going from pencil to charcoal and on to painting with oil or acrylic. I became fairly good at it but never as good as my mother. I must relate an interesting story relative to my mother, whom we called Sara the Painter lovingly, as she did a lot of artwork. We did not go to the racetrack very often, but Donna's dad, who loved the sport of kings, invited us to join him. Looking through the program for that day—I guess you call it a racing form (that's what Nathan of Detroit in *Guys and Dolls* called it)—we came upon a horse called Sara Painter. "Well," said I. "Yep," said Donna. She was a natural for us. To make a long story short, the nag came in first (the first time and only time in her career). I remember that event to this day.

The next and perhaps the most significant activity for me was learning how to use a personal computer. Remember, this was back in the late 1980s when the Internet was mainly a university tool. But thanks to my dear neighbor Marty and my first computer called Leading Edge, I was in fact on the learning curve and leading edge of a change in my medical career. I was not prepared to bow out of a medical life and became interested in administrative medicine. Then, as now, it was called *managed care.*

Donna understood this transition and knew without doubt that I would remain a patient advocate no matter what aspect of medicine I was in. She was worried about our future, I am sure. My being home all the time did not always give her the space she needed, and there were now financial concerns. Through it all, she made it easier for me psychologically to transition into a new life. I think she within herself knew that I loved medicine and hated leaving all my patients. It did not affect our relationship, and as I said before, we weathered the tide and storms together.

What managed care is can be very complex to understand. By definition, managed care is a health-care system with administrative control over primary health-care services in medical group practice. The intention is to eliminate redundancy of services and protect medical resources (primarily to reduce costs). Health education and preventive medicine are emphasized. The system of managed care evolved after World War II from the traditional fee-for-service, in which the patient paid the physician directly for services performed through a shift toward health-insurance organizations, which paid physicians and hospitals from premiums paid by the patients to the insurers—Blue Cross was one of the first—to the government programs, such as Medicare and Medicaid, which were born in the 1960s. In the 1980s, another economic shift, originated in California, led to the concept of health maintenance organizations (HMOs), with large corporations negotiating with groups of health-care workers for financing of medical and hospital expenses of the corporation's employees. HMOs also began enrolling individual patients and by the mid-1990s challenged the survival of the traditional insurance system. In polite terms, it is a medical philosophy in which the goal is a system that delivers quality, cost-effective health care by monitoring and recommending utilization of services, as well as controlling the cost of those services. It is precisely the monitoring of services that has riled many a doctor and in some cases forced early retirement. The system was run initially by nurses and administrators. There were very few doctors. That has changed to a large degree today. Again, I do not wish to be political or discuss Obamacare or the plight and future of American medicine. At the onset of managing care, much of the savings came from shortening hospital stays. I remember the old days when my grandfather had a heart attack and had to be in the hospital for six weeks. Most surgical procedures required at least one week or more. People were told that they had so many days to remain in the hospital. As I promised, this memoir includes humor, and this section is no exception, so here goes.

Three doctors unfortunately die at the same moment and arrive at the pearly gates attended by St. Peter. The holy gatekeeper told these physicians that there was a process and quality to what his job entailed. In essence, he could not let them flood the gates of heaven as they seemed to do down below where business always seems to be booming.

"Let me hear from you one by one," said St. Peter.

The first doctor aggressively pushed himself in front of his colleagues. He said, "I am a surgeon. I have with my skill and scalpel saved many a life. There are many people who but for my skill could be standing before you right now."

Recognizing that this pompous man also was righteous and did his job well, he allowed him to enter first.

The next doctor was less aggressive but was humble and self-assured. As he related his story, he spoke of his years in practice, which was often multigenerational from grandparents to the latest family members. He had delivered many babies, treated many sore throats, did minor surgery, and above all gave of himself to all. St. Peter looked very kindly at this noble man and invited him to enter.

There was a line building up now of others who had died, but there was still the last doctor to be processed through the gates of heaven. This doctor seemed humble but a bit nervous in front of his other colleagues. Kindly, St. Peter asked him, "What is it that you have done with your career?"

The doctor tried to explain his job and mentioned the words *managed care*. His job was not biblical as in who shall live or who shall die; it was more of who can stay and who has to leave. St. Peter, who as of late had heard of this term and the number of recent arrivals resultant from this new-fangled idea, started to think to himself. Recognizing that this man unknowingly had sent heaven quite a few customers of late but was honest in his belief that what he was doing was right and that he served a good purpose tried to think of an appropriate reply.

Now, some of you might not know that St. Peter had a great sense of humor. He was certainly going to let this doctor enter but could not avoid a good kibbutz. St. Peter looked at the man with great sincerity (but with great anticipation for his own moment of frivolity) saying: "You may enter heaven, dear Doctor, but you only have three days and then you have to leave. Of course, we have an appeal process."

Let me end this section with the following:

A Time for Everything

There is a time for everything,
and a season for every activity under the heavens:
To everything there is a season,
a time for every purpose under the sun.
A time to be born and a time to die;
a time to plant and a time to pluck up that which is planted;
a time to kill and a time to heal …
a time to weep and a time to laugh;
a time to mourn and a time to dance …
a time to embrace and a time to refrain from embracing;
a time to lose and a time to seek;
a time to rend and a time to sew;
a time to keep silent and a time to speak;
a time to love and a time to hate;
a time for war and a time for peace.
(Ecclesiastes 3:1–8)

Truthfully, the blows of life have not released me from the pangs of loss at each stage of my life. The greatest loss is yet to be told.

Chapter 19

• •

Regrets, We Had a Few

The natural song selection for this chapter is "My Way" made popular by Frank Sinatra and written by Paul Anka.

> Regrets, I've had a few;
> But then again, too few to mention.
> I did what I had to do
> And saw it through without exemption.

As you by now suspect, we were of humankind with all of its faults and frailties. Yes, Donna would smile and I would fret (anxiety and depression). There were many reasons. Stephen Sondheim wrote a song called "Lament," expressing remorse as to one's inability to shield others who don't listen or refuse to learn (we think so, that is, but life's lessons are pretty powerful and that bitter medicine of experience is also quite powerful). He ended his song saying that "Children can only grow from something you love to something you lose." Another way of expressing this is that God puts them under your care for a short while. You have hopes, thoughts, and dreams. As said in German, "Mann tracht und

Gott Lacht"; in other words, man proposes, and God disposes. Now in our sixties, life went on for Donna and me. We had learned much from self-help and coming to grips with acceptance. The perfect life was not ours, but it was still our life together. I must admit that going through these stages of life from anger and depression to acceptance and letting go was very hard to do. And we each had our own regrets, and some that were shared.

I have to speak for her, but I know that Donna had many regrets and dissatisfactions with life. It was not kind to her body, which was slowly ravaged by her severe arthritis, eventually rendering her unable to keep up an active life. She was not happy with herself and her self-image at times. But I would categorize much of her anguish as about her loved ones and her perceived loss of dreams and expectations of what might have been. I don't know if she ever came to full acceptance. Let me try to summarize for her (as I see it).

Our first son went out on his own very early in life and eventually left home. This to me is reminiscent of the parable of the prodigal son but without a happy outcome. The prodigal son is the story of a forgiving father. I have had a hard time coming to grips with this situation. In my section of regrets, I will refer to this using the words of another, as I am without voice to share this regret. I am still filled with great sadness. I love all my children to this day.

Our second son was a loving child and seemed to be on the straight and narrow. As mentioned, he is artistic and designed our family crest, which I cherish to this day. He was also the one who always liked being with his mom and dad. I remember all the fun we had with the sporting events we attended for many years.

Soon after his graduation from high school, Ken suddenly disappeared, leaving his home as well as his parents. Both of us were very worried. When I worry, I panic and usually get into my car and just drive aimlessly. Whether this is a premonition or not, one day, I exhibited the same behavior pattern and once again got into my car. Did Providence intervene on that given day? I shall never know. I searched aimlessly that morning, and as I was crossing a diagonal street, I suddenly had a tire blow out. As soon as I could, I pulled off on a street that I'd never heard of. Lo and behold, glory be, there was my son Ken and his friend packing his car and getting ready to leave. I was so stunned I simply said, "Good-bye," and went home. Only later on did we find a note that he had left us pinned to his bedroom wall. He was off to California, the sort of "Go West, young man" that I never realized he would be. I really think he did not like the cold weather in the Midwest.

But this adventure did not last very long. I was in a panic, developed high blood pressure, and waited to hear bad news. This episode was very difficult to handle, but the stronger partner (Donna) came to the rescue in a very practical and well-thought-out way. She always found the right solution at the right moment. With the help of a cousin in California and his older brother, we brought him home, as he had no job and soon realized that the Golden State was not so.

Well, if the left coast (California) didn't work out, maybe the East Coast would. He and a friend influenced their respective mothers to allow them to live in Florida, with the idea that Ken would attend school. I fully realize that not everyone is college material and that life's experiences can be the best teacher. My dad used to call that the college of hard knocks. How prophetic! As it worked out this time, our son is a Floridian to this very day. Donna's regret was the loss of her family, piece by piece, and that she could not see Ken on a regular basis. His start in Florida led to quite a few hard knocks, but my resilient son made it. He has a significant other, whom he has lived with for many years and a full family through her. Donna really regretted that Ken never had a child of his own. The reason for that is unknown to me and one of the things that we never understood. We thought that he would settle down into a traditional marriage. But Ken remains a loving, caring son. May he be blessed for that always.

With regards to our daughter, I think the regret is one not entirely expected at the time. Donna looked forward to having Cheryl around to help keep the home fires burning and to have a mother-daughter relationship where they could share in each other's lives. Of course, that relationship is one of the most complex on earth. Cheryl did get married in 1989, and she and her husband lived within reach of us for several years. Cheryl had a nice career and a good job. Her husband's mother was into wedding arrangements and arranged their wedding. Being a little aggressive, she left the mother of the bride out of decision making. Donna, ever the diplomat, went along with this but was clearly unhappy.

Several years later, the business was moving to Las Vegas, and once again, Donna and I were powerless when her mother-in-law suggested that the young couple relocate as well. So child number three flew the coop, so to speak. We were empty nesters with nary a chick around our table. Donna was very upset with this new loss; she always sought for a mother-daughter relationship. We could not talk her out of this move. It did not affect our marriage because we had more time for ourselves.

After seven years, Cheryl's marriage ended in a divorce. This is, of course, not uncommon, as in the United States 40 to 50 percent of all first marriages, and 60 percent of second marriages will end in divorce. According to experts, the most common reasons people give for their divorce are insecurity, lack of commitment, too much arguing, infidelity, marrying too young, unrealistic expectations, lack of equality in the relationship, lack of preparation for marriage, and abuse. This has been popularized in a 1955 film *The Seven Year Itch*, where a married man struggles with the temptation to leave his wife and small child to run off with the young woman next door, played by Marilyn Monroe. The title of the film refers to a time in a marriage when—according to the US Census Bureau—a divorce is most likely to happen.

Anyhow, Cheryl came home in 1996, and boy were we in for a surprise (this time not a regret but a joy).

Basically, my regrets match Donna's as far as our children. But in addition, my regret is not heeding that song about the changing times and not adapting to their growing up. I still wanted to play "Super Dad" and knew nothing about the concept of tough love. I also regret that most of our arguments were about our differences in raising our kids. She loved them equally but had a wiser viewpoint as to how to handle the situations that came up. I simply kept buying them things, enabling them and not letting them grow.

In a sense, giving too much is a retrospective regret. One year, we bought the boys two new shiny Schwinn bicycles. One day, as in many days before, they left them on a sidewalk, not on our property. As I asked them to put their things away, I looked outside and the new bikes were missing and two older bikes were in their place. Is this another premonition, or were we just lucky? Dad got into his car, as he was wont to do for all major or minor crises. Something compelled me to take a certain pathway, and believe it or not, several miles from our home, there were the two new bikes. All was well, and I would say that the kids who stole the bikes were careless in hiding their crime. For you nonbelievers, it perhaps can be called extraordinary luck.

As far as our extended family, Donna was also not happy with other relationships that weren't as close as she would have liked. Both of Donna's brothers and a close first cousin ended their first marriages in divorce. It is so noted that Donna remained close to the woman and the "first wives club." She also emotionally supported her younger brother's offspring more than her own brother did. The lasting regret to her dying day was that we lived so close but were miles apart from her nephew and nieces emotionally. They always say that attending a funeral and portraying a somber appearance is too late and too little. Since this is our memoir, I am not going to analyze this any further, as the responsible parties must in truth and honesty come to grips with this.

Around 1996, there was a subtle change in her behavior. She gave up large group functions and kept our social life toned down to meeting with friends on a one-to-one basis or as couples going to a movie or to dinner. I was content to get home and did not worry or care about social engagements. She was more into television programs to the wee hours and listening to her favorite genre of music, country. I think the honesty of the lyrics spoke to her. I do remember going to a few concerts with her to hear the music she loved so well. I at the same time could get some relief from sitting at the piano, composing music (usually sad and a reflection of how I felt). I would say we were individually not as happy as before. She could smile through it all, but that ability left me. When pressed by others regarding my frowns, I always replied I was smiling on the inside, but in truth, I was just living it day by day. As an aside, maybe she regretted marrying me instead of her first boyfriend, the

Tennessee waltz thief or the businessman from another city in Illinois. I don't think so, and I hope that is not true.

The best thing for me was that it never led to our breaking away from each other. At that time, I may have been a little more in tune with her feelings, but I don't think it was the right amount of sensitivity. She meant more to me than my medical practice, though my practice contains another area of regret for me.

Pablo Casal said, "In modern business, it is not the crook that is to be feared most; it is the honest man who doesn't know what he is doing." I should have thought this out carefully, as I was always honest and always independent, and this turned out to be another of my regrets.

There were two periods of time when I took in some medical practice partners. The first time lasted two weeks when Donna and I left on a vacation. Coming back, I was given notice that this was too hard a job for him and he quit.

The second time, I took in two younger doctors who brought nothing to the practice with them but saw my patients and shared in my income. One was a schemer with many ideas, none of which he fully supported and none that came to fruition. When I got sick, partner number two cancelled our insurance, as the rates had gone up for our small group. I was always independent in my solo practice but made the move thinking I could have a better life-work balance and spend some time at home, especially quality time with Donna. Samuel Goldwyn, the movie mogul, once said, "I was always independent, even when I had partners." The one issue was that I needed to give every patient my personal attention. I had invested a great deal of my life building the practice and nurturing my patients. Having partners actually took that away from me. I was working harder and spending even more hours at work. Donna was very unhappy with this attempt to make our life easier, which in actuality made it harder. She never could become close with these physicians, and we did not socialize with them.

Many people have regrets, but I have always tried to take it a step further. One must admit to God, to another person, and to oneself the nature of one's wrongs or to put it differently take an honest inventory. The following explains this in the form of an admission, acceptance, or coming to terms with our life together. Perhaps this was inspired by realization that self-inventory in an honest manner was essential. This was written many years after our being in self-help; if I recall, it was about 1998 or 1999. Donna and I were sixty-five years old.

To Thine Own Self Be True

It's hard to be true to myself, the hardest thing I have to do.
The castle stone they label Blarney, is what I pay lip service too.
I tried to impress my own self, with powers and duties galore.
I don't have to look into me, when I padlock the honesty door.

It's easy to pass over faults, looking deeply at those of another.
While making the rules and decrees, in spite of the fact that they smother.
In this way, I don't have to see the things that I really must measure.
I don't have to change things in me, those traits that I secretly treasure.
It's easy to weigh and assess, all others who bring me to grief.
For blaming my woes on another is ego protective belief.

By playing the captain or helmsman, I make others tow at the line.
While issuing laws and decrees, I'm in deep water much of the time.
Whether parent or spouse, or the boss, with each role there is a cost.
The victim I often become, my own freedom and honesty lost.

So, beware of the web that you weave, beware of the trap that you set.
Beware of the things you command, they summon a terrible debt.
Beware of the things that you do, it's sometimes harmful you see.
Beware of the message you send, you can't go it alone without me.

The jailer must guard every door, the pleader must tire of voice.
The enabler must settle each debt, the crier forgets to rejoice.
The doer must do for another, leaving little to call one's own.
The planter of gifts often reaps, the dependency seeds he has sown.
The sigher forgets how to smile, the judge only thinks of the fees.
The person who lives in denial often loses true vision you see.

The list of our titles is mighty, the roles we assume are immense.
Much of our true self is lost, reality merged with pretense.
The games that I play must be over, my mind and I all agree.
It's time to put me together, all my self-worth is crying to be

Free of burdens created by habits and defects I'm trying
to mend.
Though changing often in subtle, it's the only way I can amend.

Through courage and wisdom both gathered, the things I
have learned can astound.
Through the power of people around me, for many have
walked the same ground.
I'll face my life in a new way, where others know what
I'm about.
In a word, let me be me, the only role no one will doubt.

So you see, I am making amends to all those I thought had hurt
Donna as she expressed in her regrets and I expressed in mine. Family
squabbles and her siblings' problems weighed heavily on her. During
these times, she let people know how she honestly felt and wrote a
few letters that I bet she could have taken back. I, in turn, backed her
completely but might have taken another approach, as one can't always
retract what is recorded in a letter. We are all human and have our own
perspectives, viewpoints, and lives to live.

A final and most important regret is that my ears were open but
my mind was often closed. I should have listened with my heart and
to the truth within me earlier on in life. When you are married or
committed to someone in your life, it can't be my way; has to be *our*
way. From the beginning on, one must learn to listen more keenly, to
communicate more, and to agree to agree on decisions that affect more
than your own life or your will to control or manage things in your
own way. The lessons that life taught me were sincerity, openness, and
communication, and it took me a long time to get there.

Both Donna and I forgave a lot but had problems forgetting. This led to a new, evolving relationship between Donna and me. I started to be more open with her and not do things behind her back (i.e., giving money to our children). I also could speak more openly with her if I was truthful. I knew that she knew that I kept things from her, and yet she remained silent until the truth emerged. It was a relief when she always forgave me instead of hiding her tears. We built a new relationship based on more communication and understanding.

The key to a relationship is to keep the door open, meaning communicating rather than letting it well up inside. The road to be traveled must be a shared pathway. One can retain one's own uniqueness and independence, but the road must be sojourned together. One must remember that little things mean a lot. I don't mean flowers and chocolates; I mean a hug, an embrace, a gentle touch, and words that need to be spoken.

I guess that were I to be completely honest, I could have enjoyed my life's pathway as much, if not more, if I had chosen to be a musician and a writer. I would not have wanted to change anything else, my children, my family, and my wife for sure. I'm grateful for the special lady who was granted to me. She shared my life with lots of love and gave it meaning and dignity; for you see, she was my soul mate and my friend along life's difficult road. She knew me well and always knew just what to say.

Life in a way is like a storybook that you open, a key to a door or a road to be traveled. In a storybook of real life, there is comedy and tragedy. You can't be the only character as life plays out. One is not the author or director but a sharing participant. These are some of the lessons that I learned.

Chapter 20

. . . .

Leaving

At last I can see life has been patiently waiting for me
And I know there's no guarantees, but I'm not alone
When all you can see are the years passing by
And I have made up my mind that those days are gone . . .
—Rascal Flatts

This is a sad part of our memoir. I could just as easily have referred to Stephen Foster: "Gone are the days, when my heart was young and gay. Gone are my friends from the cotton fields away." You remember my relating the fact that my dad gave us the down payment on our home. I also told you that I could not repay him then. Even on his deathbed, he asked me to be sure and take care of Mother and Donna, and I did. With Donna's initiative, we moved Mother from her small apartment to a condominium that we paid for. How happy we were for her knowing that she would meet many new friends, and that she did. She also remained active as the president of a Hadassah group, for years and years, as no one wanted to replace her.

Now as before, our combined relatives were succumbing to age and illness, so it was with my mother. She had always had an erratic heartbeat, a condition called atrial fibrillation, and a bad heart murmur probably caused by rheumatic fever. I don't remember the exact date but in 1994, she was vacationing with a friend in Florida when I received a call from a hotel doctor. My mom was in congestive heart failure. I asked that she be sent home as soon as possible so that Donna and I could be at her side. It turned out that she had ruptured a heart valve and needed urgent valve replacement. We chose a heart surgeon of excellence, and she went through the surgery successfully.

Now here is the humor of the situation. This nice Jewish mom of mine was given a porcine (pig) valve as a replacement. We joked about it but were thankful that she was well. It is about that time that she took a liking to Chinese food (who in our family didn't), and the special dish she liked had beef with peapods. I could never bring myself to tell her that the very tasty sauce was oyster sauce, as she had been kosher all of her life. I was thankful that she would eat out, and I did not want to tell her about the sauce.

After her recovery on a Mother's Day, we took my mom to see a play. While leaving the theater, she developed extreme pain in her groin and right hip, almost to the point of collapsing. Within a short time, it was discovered that she had lung cancer, which had spread to her bones. There was little we could do from a treatment standpoint, and she passed away September 22, 1995. Donna and I were both sixty-one years old at that time.

As to the important women who shaped my life, this point in my story now has taken two of them away from me, my beloved grandmother and my great mom. She indeed was the crown of the good person. I miss her deeply.

This song by Stephen Foster typifies my anguish about the years gone by and belief that the good years were gone. After Mom died September 22, 1995, we had to sell her condominium. The real estate person said that she was moving into a new area in a suburb north of Chicago. At that time, I had to travel from the city to Arlington Heights, Illinois, and later on to Itasca, Illinois, for my job. This was a lengthy trip, occupying many hours of the day. Each day, I had to return, passing by the house my mother had lived in, causing me a great deal of emotion.

One time, I received a call from an emergency room that my wife was in a car accident while I was at work. I had to go from Itasca to a hospital in Skokie, Illinois, miles and miles away. I don't know how long it took me to get there, but my mind wandered into the worst scenario. Thankfully, she was all right, but I never wanted to be that far away from her again. That to me was the most compelling reason to move——so that I would never be that far away from her again.

Saying good-bye to our dear friends on Jarlath was hard to do. I think at this moment of that beautiful song that Donna loved so much: "Time to Say Good-bye."

> When I'm alone
> I dream on the horizon and words fail;
> yes, I know there is no light in a room
> where the sun is not there ...
> (Andrea Bocelli and Sarah Brightman)

This was now 1997, and Donna and I were sixty-three years old.

For me, as a depressed dreamer, I felt that there was little light in the tunnel at that time. I wanted to move, thinking that there was a geographical cure for things that ailed me. I must say Donna did not readily agree. Our home was her castle, and she was content to remain there forever. Being the good wife she always was, she agreed to look around on weekends for homes on sale. I know she was placating me.

The real estate agent who had sold my mother's condominium had just purchased a lot in a new development and asked if Donna would like to see it. She remarked that she would love to have us as neighbors. Donna agreed to look at the models. My dear Donna astounded me by putting down a deposit on a lot in the suburb we were to live in. Why she succumbed so easily is unknown to me. In part, she felt my discontent in general and gave in to me. I could not read her mind. I think she was unhappy to leave our beautiful home. I wish now that she had put her foot down, but she tried to please me. I think I hurt her deeply.

This was to be our first experience in building a home from scratch. Let me correct that statement. It was a house, not a home. Our home and only home over thirty years was on the street that I now call our beloved Jarlath. I have come to the opinion that a home is a home when it is passed on and lived in from generation to generation. At that time, the next generation was out of the nest and I had to let that illusion go.

I will never forget the day we were all packed up waiting for the furniture movers. I had second thoughts, but in truth, Donna left her heart and soul there. She sat there for hours, nary a thought or word spoken. I realized then but more so now that a piece of her was dying. All the years we lived in our new house, she never thought it was just right, as she was always comparing it to our home.

We moved to our new house on March 14, 1997. Our daughter came home from Las Vegas, leaving her life with her husband temporarily to help us move. The first day we moved in, I was helping to move some boxes when I suddenly felt dizzy and temporarily lost the sight in one eye. Some of you may think this was emotional; some may choose to think that it was a punishment for pulling Donna away from the street she loved. As it turned out, the heavy lifting had released plaque from a neck artery to my eye. Fortunately, it did not lead to a stroke or visual loss.

There were no more dear friends and neighbors close by to visit. It was a rather sterile community with suburban streetlighting and a place where the sidewalks rolled up at an early hour. Donna, with her unique talents, made our new house as beautiful and open as always to everyone. Everyone turned out to be her grade school and high school friends, and some of our acquaintances, but mainly her dear friends. They know who they are!

Yes, the beguine was still playing, and our dance of life was still on. It was, however, at a different pace, slowing down measurably. There may have been chances wasted in earlier days. Donna's arthritis was getting very bad. We should have, in healthier and younger days, taken more time away from the mundane and looked for more excitement. I take the major blame for this because my practice meant a lot to me and my disinterest in travel or new activities was apparent. Donna, through no fault of hers, was becoming very arthritic, and at times, she bravely tried to manage our social life. I truly wasted a chance to be more sincere, to listen more, and to be in touch with the needs of my wife. I think I was happier than she was. I was closer to work and liked my job. She could not get out as often to be with her friends; she slept longer into the morning hours, while not sleeping well at night. We ultimately gave up going to as many concerts, plays, and all exciting things. Our main social activity was dining with friends and certain family members.

From that day on, the smile remained, but a part of her was lost. She continued her beautiful needlepoint works, and we had fun finding a shop in our new neighborhood selling the canvases and threads that were needed. Within her heart, however, there were shattered threads. At this time, her arthritis got worse, her energy diminished, and there were times when she needed to remain in bed for hours or days at a time. At other times, she developed severe insomnia. However, she was into needlepoints depicting lovely ladies. To me, that was a reflection of her good soul.

In 2004, when we were seventy years old, another crisis hit us. I was having difficulty with a prostate problem and assumed it was part of the aging process. They say that a doctor who treats himself has a fool for a physician. How true that turned out to be. When I finally saw a urologist, he found that a certain test called prostate specific antigen (PSA) was higher than it should be. I felt that this was due to infection and tried some antibiotics. After a few months, it was clear that this test was rising and it was time to have a biopsy done. Within a few days, I learned that I had prostate cancer. I saw a specialized surgical oncologist and elected to have major surgery. This was very frightening for Donna as well as me. I must tell you about her devotion to me. She decided to take a hotel room minutes away from the hospital so that she could be near me and spend as much time as possible with me when I was hospitalized. One can see her devotion to me through this latest illness. My concern when I was in the hospital was that she was safely back at the hotel. I had to call her each evening to make sure she was safe. She was my concern.

One can also tell that the outcome was good, as I am here today free of cancer.

We returned to Jarlath Street on many occasions to visit our friends and once again participate in the block parties. I never, although invited, could walk into my old home and retreated instead to the homes of Barbara and Irene. I must admit that when we left, I was a bit sad and felt then as I do now that I made a mistake. I hope my wife is hearing this.

This poem is a way of making amends to her for many reasons, including moving from the home she loved. It is also a need to express in truth that I may have been a little selfish and insensitive. It was written after our move and sometime after my recovery from cancer. I was once again very introspective. The date was 2008, as I recall. Donna and I were now seventy-four years old.

AMENDS
Please don't change a hair for me.
How old that still stale line.
If none of us would ever change.
How boring the design.
If you really care for life.
And for the folks you meet.
You have to learn to modify.
And lose that old conceit.

Amendments are additions.
They add something to your life.
To live without conditions.
Makes you free from lots of strife.
My inner soul has always known.

The pain it dare not show.
That foolish pride has done me harm
While letting problems grow.

There are many ways to make amends.
It's not difficult to do.
You first must learn to like yourself.
And think the best of you.
Practice smiles and cheerful thoughts.
A tender touch, a grin.
Learn to listen, don't advise.
It's quite a deadly sin.

Each of us must find our path.
On which we'll try to stay.
To learn a better way to live
And learn to love, to lend an ear.
And live the Golden rule
Remember, no one's perfect.
I guess I played the fool.

Yes, the path I chose for us was wrong. I should have listened with my heart. If but I could have her back (and that is but a dream), the right path would lead us back to Jarlath, her friends, and the better parts of her life.

My darling, I am sorry!

Chapter 21

Revival

(Chorus)
And you
Light up my life.
You give me hope
To carry on.
—Joe Brooks, "You Light Up My Life"

Life went on as usual but at a much slower pace. You could say that our dance of life continued but was more of a two-step, slow and easy. Let me add a few details. My mom became ill. After successful valve replacement, within a few months, she developed her lung cancer.

Cheryl had come to visit and to be with her grandmother until she took her last breath in 1995. At that time, she looked tired and we asked her to stay. She chose not to do so and returned to Las Vegas after we moved to our new home. A year or so later, upon needing separation from a failing marriage, she came home to us in late 1996 and found herself a job. Donna was happy as a robin filling its nest once again. Things went along well, but in my mind, because we had no grandchildren and with our daughter's divorce proceedings, I felt we would never have a grandchild.

One Saturday in July 1997, we were leaving to visit some friends but saw our daughter was having some abdominal cramps. She told us not to worry and to go on with our visit. She looked fine to us, so we agreed to leave.

When at our friend's home, I kept talking about having a grandchild. Well, as it turned out, there was Cheryl, at home, all alone and delivering a baby girl without a midwife or doctor. She had no clue at that time that she was pregnant, and we could see no difference in her body appearance. She also was having normal female physiological habits. Our daughter is a very bright girl, and she was able to deliver as in ancient times, all by herself. She was also keen enough to wrap the baby, keeping her on her chest and calling the paramedics.

When we got home that evening, there was a note on our front door that Cheryl had delivered a baby girl and was at Highland Park Hospital where they completed separation of mother and child. We, of course, rushed to the hospital to see our daughter and her daughter. Was this a premonition or a gift from above? My daughter's view was that of denial and disbelief, since her difficult separation from her husband in their seventh year of marriage. Our granddaughter, Sara, was born July 12, 1997.

Donna helped her daughter in every way to raise this baby. She once again had a smile of happiness. The time came to name the child. When my mother was yet alive, she told Cheryl that should she have a daughter, it must be named after her. My mother's name was Sara Rose, and the baby of course became Sara Rose.

I think it was meant to be beshert (you now know the word from another chapter), a happy ending of an unhappy marriage with a little help from the angels above. Do you believe in angels? I do! When Sara was young, I would sing an old Welsh tune and a Hebrew tune to her about angels. Here are a few lines.

The following is from the Welsh "All through the Night." The Welsh lyrics were written by John Ceiriog Hughes and have been translated into several languages, including English (most famously by Harry Boulton) and Breton. One of the earliest English versions was by Thomas Oliphant in 1862.

Sleep my child and peace attend thee,
All through the night
Guardian angels God will send thee,
All through the night
Soft the drowsy hours are creeping
Hill and vale in slumber sleeping,
I my loving vigil keeping
All through the night.

The next is from the Hebrew "Shalom Aleichem." "Shalom Aleichem" is a traditional song sung Friday night at the beginning of Shabbat, the Jewish Sabbath, welcoming the angels who accompany a person home on the eve of the Sabbath. This liturgical poem was written by the kabbalists of Safed in the late sixteenth or early seventeenth century.

Peace upon you, ministering angels, messengers of the
Most High,
of the Supreme King of Kings, the Holy One, blessed be He.
Come in peace, messengers of peace, messengers of the
Most High,
of the Supreme King of Kings, the Holy One, blessed be He.
Bless me with peace, messengers of peace, messengers of
the Most High,
of the Supreme King of Kings, the Holy One, blessed be He.
May your departure be in peace, messengers of peace,
messengers of the Most High,
of the Supreme King of Kings, the Holy One, blessed be He.

It was also for Donna in her end time when I would croon this
into her ears using the original Hebrew. She did not acknowledge this
directly to me but told a caregiver that her husband was serenading
her in Yiddish, which I was not. Donna never spoke Yiddish and had
only a smattering knowledge of Hebrew. I was praying in Hebrew for
celestial intervention.

As many of Donna's friends noticed, Donna revived dramatically
and our dance of life transitioned back to a fox-trot, a ballroom dance
in 4/4 time, with an alternation of two slow and two quick steps. The
slow steps, a part of her aging processes and arthritis, were necessary.
However, her granddaughter, Sara, was her hope and dream realized.

My role in those early days was to love Sara, and my overprotectiveness
reappeared. When family and friends came to call, there was I at the
head of the crib, not letting anyone get too close. Incidentally, she was
the best-dressed baby and young child ever, thanks to her grandmother.

The Thought of Grandparents
Loneliness had been mine to that day
For things thought never to be.
But now it seems so long ago.
Now you are ours you see.

And so she was ours to have and to hold and a chance to raise a child and do it all over again. For we were second parents so to speak, caring for Sara when her mom worked weekends. This revived Donna dramatically, as she again assumed the role of caring for a baby and watching her grow.

We had a chance to revisit walking, talking, and toilet training as she was growing up in our happy household. It was our second time around. Let me try to recapitulate those memories that I have of our grandparenting/shared-parenting role.

I must have forgotten what little girls like at first, because my first presents were Hot Wheels (tiny racing cars and vehicles of all sorts). Maybe this could have been satisfying the inner child in me. I also bought her a tiny train set with a small round track. An early present was a basketball game played with a table tennis ball that would catapult into a tiny net.

Of course, the little train set evolved into Thomas the Tank Engine and its full complement of trains, complex tracks, and a large table to keep it on. There were all sorts of supplemental products that one would see around the railroad and surrounding town. I think that I enjoyed this immensely (probably my second childhood).

Later on, there were outdoor toys, such as little houses to walk through, a small ladder that I thought would be safe until my Sara fell off and broke an arm. Of course, there was the progression from small bikes to larger ones.

From the very start, I knew the importance of learning computer skills. Of course, her expertise today is well beyond mine. We started out with colors and shapes and progressed on to more complex computer games. I'm very proud that I laid the foundation for her.

In time, we began to go in the right direction—oh boy, did we ever. Sara had the largest collection of bears, a wonder to be seen. Wherever we went, I always purchased a toy bear or two for her. We eventually graduated to the Build-a-Bear product where she selected a bear, stuffed it, gave it a heart, and then clothed it in style. There is an interesting story regarding the bears. She named every one and never forgot a single name. She invented a game called bear school, and I was lucky to be the assistant teacher. I usually stumbled on quite a few names only to be corrected by my granddaughter. In retrospect, those were great times.

Other collections included many different kinds of dolls, from Barbie to Bratz, and on to the American Girl doll collectibles. The dolls of course needed full apparel. I left doll play mainly to her girlfriend who lived next door. One thing that amused me was that the neighbor child would always behead the dolls and remove their shoes. (Was she in her earlier incarnation part of the French Revolution? We'll never know!)

One evening, Donna and I were sitting in the den when little Sara walked in wearing a hat. We had many hats lying around the house, and Sara had chosen one that was not her own. We thought that this was cute. We giggled and went back to what we were doing. A few minutes later, in she comes with another hat, and then another, each time playacting and hamming it up. This was very reminiscent of her creative mom and the Halloween story. This game then became a regular part of Sara's repertoire.

These next sentiments explain the relationship between Donna and Sara. I chose to express this in Sara's own words.

"There are a lot of great things that I remember about Bubbe. Specifically, I remember watching TV with her at night. After my mom and grandpa (Zayde) went to sleep, I would run downstairs to spend time with Bubbe. We would watch several different TV shows, such as game shows, the *AFV* (*America's Funniest Videos*), and the Ellen DeGeneres show. We would share a chocolate bar and a bottle of Diet Pepsi as we watched.

"Thursdays were nail days. Fridays were hair days. Every time I had off of school, I would go with her to get a manicure. She always helped me choose a great color. Then, we would go out to eat. I remember Bubbe went to my in-school field trip about the Civil War in sixth grade. We ate lunch in the lunchroom but had to leave early because my braces were ripping the inside of my mouth. Bubbe convinced the difficult office lady to allow us to leave."

We took little trips quite often. At first, our trips where local, such as heading to learning museums and to a place that she loved called Lamb's Farm, where challenged children were given jobs and a place to live. She loved seeing all the animals and playing miniature golf on a tiny course. There was also a train ride through the park that she loved every time we visited.

Then, there was a special farm in a nearby suburb, called Diddier's farm, where I'm sure many generations had visited. We usually went there at harvest time and during Halloween. There were rides through the cornfields, a haunted house, and of course animals. Here is an interesting story. There was a feeding pit where one could feed young animals. Sara and animals always have had an affinity for each other, and I got to share in the joy of feeding them. We walked in and were immediately greeted by goats and lambs that jumped on us. Can you imagine what we looked like and smelled like?

There was another place called the Grove. The Grove is 135 acres of ecologically diverse prairie grove land preserved and maintained by the Glenview Park District. The Grove was the home of visionary horticulturist and educator Dr. John Kennicott, who brought his family from New Orleans to settle on this land in 1836. It was here that Dr. John's son Robert Kennicott loved nature, exhibiting the plant and native specimens of our native Illinois. I remember our pleasant walks through the grove, visiting a wigwam and a shared Native American dwelling as well as the log cabins early settlers lived in. The Grove was designated a National Historic Landmark by the US Department of the Interior in 1976. It is on the National Registry of Historic Places. The Grove is a partner with the US Fish and Wildlife Service and Chicago Wilderness as well. Sara at first loved playing near the turtle pond but was scared every time she looked up. There before her was a giant stuffed black bear. Imagine her afraid of a *bear*.

Of course, local trips turned into more distant places. Being our grandchild, she had to experience cruising. Sara went on several trips with us to Alaska, to the Caribbean, and to Eastern and Western Mexico, and she loved every minute being together with her mom and grandparents. During these trips, Sara and I had to visit every floor and every nook and cranny of each ship we were on. She did not like signing up for the young people's programs. But when she did, she made several friends. Like her grandfather, she preferred the quality of a one-on-one relationship. To occupy herself, she started to write little short stories, many of which I have saved to this day. On one cruise, our tablemate asked Sara to write a story each evening, so that he could read it aloud. This gentleman was a very gregarious and extroverted guy. In a very theatrical voice, he read each story to the delight of Sara but not always to the pleasure of our fellow passengers at sea.

We were so proud of her writing skills and her ability as an actress who could play any role. Donna purchased a puppet show for her, and we were delighted with each performance. Her skill as a writer then led to her playlets, in which all of the family had to participate. I had to film Donna and Sara in her plays, with Donna playing multiple roles. She adored this time with her grandchild. It also led to her publishing two children's stories, one called "My Name Is Cindi" and "Help Me, Dianna." She was interviewed by a local newspaper, and both books are in the neighborhood library. Eventually, I know not why, but the young writer stopped producing her books, which were very insightful for a person so young. This activity ended in middle school.

These were most precious and proud times for both of us. Donna enjoyed spending time with Sara during these outings.

As in many households in America and other lands, people, especially children, adore creatures of many species. Donna allowed all creatures for Sara, something she did not do for her own kids. Lizards, frogs, guinea pigs, and hamsters were no-nos for our children, but she nodded okay for Sara. In our household, we started out with the smallest creatures, namely fish. From there, after many "burials at sea," we progressed to a lovable rodent called a hamster and had several of

them, which Donna refused to touch. Before we go on to the best of
pets, I take a moment to list the creatures we adopted into our family.

> Keke, a beta fish
> Goldie, a beta fish
> Dosapon, a minnow
> Peppermint, a minnow
> Buttons, a minnow
> Smiles, a beta fish
> Doritoes

As an aside, when the first few fish left for a better place, Sara's
mom told her that an ailing fish had to go to a fish hospital. Actually,
she tried to substitute fish similar in appearance and size to the one
that met its maker (bellied up). After a while, Sara caught on and the
ceremony of burial at sea became a common occurrence. Let us progress
to the hamsters.

> Hami
> Jacky
> Charpella
> Snowy, who escaped from her cage and disappeared
> somewhere in our home. We eventually found her
> unharmed but looking very thirsty and hungry, as any
> escapee on the loose.

There are two other pets that Sara babysat.

> Hammy, belonging to Debbie our next-door neighbor (We
> had the misfortune of having Hammy die while we were
> babysitting)

Sir Isaac Newton, a tortoise who may still be alive

To all the others, in memoriam and rest in peace.

Now onward to our best family member!
"How Much Is that Doggie in the Window?"
How much is that doggie in the window?
The one with the waggy tail.
How much is that doggie in the window?
I do hope that doggie's for sale …

Like many a child, Sara wanted a larger, more interactive pet. Like her grandfather and grandmother, she was a dog, not a cat, person. Donna loved dogs. We had three other dogs in our earlier life, Cindi the sausage dog that I rescued from a medical school lab and two beautiful Weimaraners. With the help of her financier (*moi*), Sara purchased a book about all the dog breeds, their habits, their traits, and their longevity. She really could not make up her mind. And so shortly before her tenth birthday in 2007, we found an ad for a place called PUPs for Kids. We went out there, and Sara was able to look at all the new puppies. Most of them jumped on her and nipped at her, but one beautiful caramel-and-white-colored puppy just gently followed her around. The dog found her playmate primate sister, and Sara found her canine love.

We had just celebrated the Passover season and had just read about the patriarchs and matriarchs. Sara, who carries the name of the queen of all matriarchs, chose two names for her new puppy, Leah Rachel, and we lovingly call her LeLe. She was a cockapoo. A cockapoo is a designer dog. It is the cross of an American cocker spaniel or an English cocker spaniel and a poodle (in most cases a miniature poodle or toy poodle). Of course, this was to be Sara's obligation. Leah however, became the loving ward of my daughter, Cheryl, and is to this very day. I'm not sure if Leah recognizes the alpha human in our home. She is loving and protective to all. When I used to walk her, if a neighbor or neighbor dog approached me, she would plant herself squarely before me. If a stranger or relative approached our home, Leah would let out her warning bark. It is so to this day. We have had many strangers, such as workmen or caretakers enter our home. When she sees that we greet them in a friendly manner, her tail begins to wag and she follows the visitors from the house in an inquisitive manner. Do I think Leah is smart? Of course I do!

Some examples of her intelligence are as follows:

She knows everyone's schedule in the house and rushes to the front window minutes before we arrive home.

She knows that the mailman or FedEx man has a treat for her, and when we are outdoors, she patiently sits at the end of the driveway waiting for her gift.

She knows that her mom owes her a treat after her morning walk and upon return rushes to me, knowing that I will support this.

She has great compassion for her family. When Donna was bedridden, she would climb on the bed and gently place her paws on her. As of recent, I have had to use a cane. She is very careful with me and watches me with great tenderness.

She knows who the center of this family is, and it is Leah.

You see, dogs have always left their pawprints on my heart. That is especially so for this beautiful animal, Leah, who is part of my family and touches me deeply every day of my life. I don't know if she remembers Donna and how she would lie next to her with her paws on Donna's frail body. I do know that she follows me everywhere and is cautious as I have lower extremity weakness and use a walking stick.

Sara, I am sure, was influenced by Donna. She loves clothing, shoes, bracelets, hair styling, and having her nails done. I'm sure that her closet is bursting with both old and new clothes, some with tags never removed. From an early age, she had a habit of twirling her hair in the same place so that at times it looked as if a bald spot would develop. This is uncanny, as my mother, whom she is named after, did the same thing and I am wont to as well at times.

My Funny Valentine

Songwriters Rodgers and Hart

She really isn't my funny valentine, but there is a little anecdote to share with you. The title I used comes from "My Funny Valentine."

> Sweet comic valentine
> You make me smile with my heart
> Your looks are laughable, unphotographable [not true, she
> is beautiful]
> Yet, you're my favorite work of art...

It goes on to say, "Don't change a hair for me" (that is the point).

You see, Sara decided to change the color of her hair to black. Sara is a natural blonde, with all different shades, and I hated to see her do this. But she is a teenager and tried this recently. I am thankful that phase is over—and please spare us tattoos or putting rings and things into her body parts. Sara, as I write this story, is now seventeen years, old, drives her grandmother's car, is soon to be a senior in high school, and then on to life wherever it takes her.

As I reflect on these times, I feel strongly about the good that came into my life as well as the bad. Life had taught me to do an exercise called a gratitude list. I used my favorite means of expressing myself to do so.

In Gratitude

In gratitude, I thank my God
For bringing me my wife
In pride and honest sharing truth
I've learned things in this life
I'm thankful that my kids have grown
I'm thankful for a friend
But most of all this loving child
My Sara helps me mend.

Chapter 22

• •

More Stories of the Road

On the road again goin' places that I've never been
Seein' things that I may never see again
And I can't wait to get on the road again …
—Willie Nelson

Our dance of life was to go on for a bit longer before the lights began to dim. Now in our midseventies, our longer trips were over. Donna at that time was a great friend of my cousin Sheila, who lived in Rancho Mirage, California. But during the Christmas holidays, when Sara was out of school, we tried to get away. We had been to California many times, visiting San Francisco, the wine country up and down the Great Sur, and much of Southern California, seeing a great deal of that lovely state. You can recall our interest in moving there that never came to pass. Well, it almost did! Donna and I, along with her brother Michael and his first wife, Judy, put a down payment down on a lovely condo in Palm Springs. To make a long story short, we never got to enjoy that as Brother Mike and his wife soon separated.

And so, we once more traveled to California during the Christmas holidays, taking Sara along, of course. The first trip was to Anaheim, and our granddaughter had a ball at Disneyland, spending time with her cousins. Donna and I and Sheila and Chuck spent time reminiscing about the good old days. They were always very hospitable and were fun to be with, so we wintered with them several times.

Here, then, is an interesting detail. Sheila still communicated with our cousin Susan. I mentioned earlier that cousin Susan was an only child. I was too, so we had something in common. Unfortunately, we had lost touch over the years, and I hardly knew her at all. Susan had lost a young child to congenital heart disease as well as her husband, Bruce, a wonderful guy. He had had several bad heart attacks and an intestinal infection needing long-term care. (Little did I know that I would soon have something else in common with her.) They had moved several times and to several states. I heard through Sheila that Susan was now remarried and living in an area near Philadelphia. I had procured Susan's telephone number, and after thinking it over when we got home, I gave her a call.

It was as if yesterday was back when I reunited with her. I promised her that we would meet again, and so we did. We made plans to visit her, and so we did. It's interesting that in my career in managed care, I spent a great deal of time in my home office in downtown Philadelphia in 2008. The context of this is that Susan and I had this affinity earlier on in life, but we had lost touch over the years. I never contacted her. Her home is in Washington Crossing, Philadelphia. She and her new husband, Elliot, met us at the airport in 2009, and it was very congenial from the start. We all hit it off, first stopping off at Redding Court, a large facility where one can munch, lunch, or dine on anything one's heart desires. Afterward, we spent a lot of time at their home, meeting their children and grandchildren. We also traveled a lot with Susan and Elliot, who chauffeured us about.

Later before leaving them, we took a trip to a fantastic institution called Constitution Center. The National Constitution Center is a one-stop civic headquarters for the people and Philadelphia's premier field-trip destination. The museum brings the story of "We the People" to life for students through a hands-on museum experience and innovative tools for teaching about the Constitution. It was interesting for the adults but was especially interesting for us watching Sara in this interactive museum.

We all should know the Constitution, and for the sake of brevity, I remind you of the preamble:

> We the People of the United States, in Order to form a more perfect Union, establish Justice, insure domestic Tranquility, provide for the common defence, promote the general Welfare, and secure the Blessings of Liberty to ourselves and our Posterity, do ordain and establish this Constitution for the United States of America.

For me, the most exciting exhibition was Signers' Hall. One of the museum's most popular and iconic attractions, Signers' Hall allowed you to walk among the Founding Fathers who added their names to the Constitution—as well as those who dissented—on September 17, 1787.

Signers' Hall brought to life for us the final day of the Constitutional Convention in the Assembly Room of the Pennsylvania State House, now known as Independence Hall. There are numerous famous faces in the room, including George Washington, Benjamin Franklin, James

Madison, and Alexander Hamilton. We posed beside our favorite Founding Fathers for a great photo op, and Sara sat on quite a few laps. She also took the oath of a federal judge, robed and all, and was given a copy of the Constitution. This July 4, I watched quite a few movies about the Constitution and the great battles regarding states' rights, opposition to a federal government, and the issues of rum, sugar, and slaves, etc. But it was signed, and all of us are in the greatest country today because of our forebears.

As we left, we promised to see each other once again, and that time soon came. Susan and Elliot were thinking of a trip to Europe, particularly England and France (London and Paris). They called us and asked if we would be their companions for a trip planned for 2010. Sick as Donna was with her arthritis, her eyes brightened, her energy returned, and I did not dissent to travel as I usually did. I had a premonition that this would be our last trip or our last fling. I was kind of anxious to see parts of the world where we had traveled when in our twenties. I did not then think that age would play such a difficult role and take its toll on both of us but especially Donna.

Donna was rejuvenated and excited. As poorly as she felt, this flow of something good happening had a positive effect. As she always did, she took part in the planning and offered some suggestions. We went shopping, and I had great joy helping her pick out some new items of clothing. My contribution, knowing that this was a long trip, was to surprise her with first-class flights abroad and then home again. I knew how cramped she would be in standard seating.

Chapter 23

● ●

Hello to Europe

There'll Always Be an England

Clarke Ross-Parker (born Albert Rostron Parker) (1914–1974) was an English pianist, composer, lyricist, and actor. He is best known for cowriting the songs "We'll Meet Again" and "There'll Always Be an England." This song was popular when England was at war and constantly bombed with V2 rockets. I remember the version sung by Vera Lynn.

> There'll always be an England
> While there's a country lane,
> Wherever there's a cottage small
> Beside a field of grain.

Yes, there will always be an England. It has been able to withstand multiple invasions, including a heavy bombing in World War II. The first time Donna and I visited London, it had rebuilt itself once again and again become a major city. We returned again to England in the 1980s and did all of the things that tourists do. When we came back this last time to London, much of it looked as it had many years earlier. Of course, we revisited and experienced the ritualistic and still exciting traditions of a country with a long-standing monarchistic and elegant establishment. We once again saw all the other sights, including Buckingham Palace, Kensington Palace, Westminster Abbey, and the beautiful parks. Lest I forget, Big Ben was still there.

What was different now was that in modern London, the financial district area was in architectural opposition to the London we remembered. Also different was the presence of people from all corners of the globe, making London like the great cities of the United States, a melting pot. Benjamin Disraeli said that London was a roost for every bird.

Another change was that England was once again under attack, this time by Islamic radical extremists. It was a bit unnerving to hear the sirens all over the city while we were there.

Donna had a great deal of difficulty walking, so this time, we hired a personal tour guide everywhere we went. I stayed close to her, fearful that she would fall on those ancient cobblestones of Europe. I know that I was very sentimental at that time and held her hand everywhere we went. When we did go outdoors, Donna would often rest on a bench. Come the evening, we did enjoy several plays, and believe it or not, the best food we found was in a little Italian restaurant in the theater district. During the day, we rested a lot but continued to experience afternoon tea. This ritual is quite different from afternoon tea or coffee anywhere else in the world. If I can recall the order of things, it was heat the pot before adding the tea, pour boiled water over the tea, and of course drink out of bone china. And of course, there were special sandwiches and biscuits. Donna and I enjoyed this while our cousins were out shopping. It seems that the best of travel buddies are those who let you do your own thing. Susan and Elliott were no exception.

For the first time, we visited the Churchill War Rooms to discover the original Cabinet War Rooms, the wartime bunker that sheltered Churchill and his government during the Blitz. We explored the various simply furnished rooms to experience the secret history that lived on underground and the stories of those who worked underground as London was being bombed above them. The Cabinet War Rooms, under a great deal of concrete, provided the secret underground headquarters for the core of the British government throughout the Second World War. The fear that London would be the target of aerial bombardment had troubled the government since the First World War, and of course, thanks to the tyrant Adolph Hitler, they were quite right. From 1940 to 1945, hundreds of men and women would spend thousands of vital hours there, and it soon became the inner sanctum of British government.

A great place where we discovered more about Churchill's life was the interactive lifeline at the center of the museum, which covers every year of Churchill's life and allows you to open documents, photos, and film clips as well as find hidden animations. Elliot, Donna, and I were all born in 1934, and we quickly selected the dates and events that happened on our birthdays.

We did travel outside of London to so many beautiful towns and villages, and we ate in some quaint restaurants. One day, we asked our tour guide if we could visit any sites where the Americans fought and died. She said it was a bit far and said, "Sorry," as the polite English person always did. Donna came up with another suggestion, which was doable. We traded away some part of the itinerary to visit a unique site that my wife had always wanted to see. She was enamored by that ancient structure at Stonehenge. I remembered seeing pictures of it, but when we arrived on that cool day, the experience was chilling, so to speak (literally, not figuratively). By that time, our very caring tour guide found a wheelchair for my lady. I will never forget the one photograph of Donna sitting in that wheelchair, all bundled up with a babushka on and the three of us behind her. Donna asked me to take pictures of Stonehenge from many angles, and I complied. One wonders why she was so excited and if this has any bearing on reincarnation and traveling souls. No one knows who built it, who carried these huge stones to that site, or what the purpose of the site was. It was there long before the Druids. To this day, however, when there is a Druid festival, the site is open to them.

Stonehenge is located in Wiltshire, England, and is one of the most recognizable and famous sites in the world. Stonehenge consists of a ring of standing stones that have fascinated archaeologists, historians, and the general public for many years. There are many different theories about when it was built, but most agree it was between 2000 and 3000 BC (five thousand years ago!). The biggest of its stones, as we learned, are known as *sarsens* and are up to 30 feet (9 meters) tall and weigh 25 tons (22.6 metric tons) on average. It is widely believed that they were brought from Marlborough Downs, a distance of 20 miles (32 kilometers) to the north. Smaller stones, referred to as *bluestones* (they have a bluish tinge when wet or freshly broken), weigh up to four tons, and most of them appear to have come from the Preseli Hills in western Wales, a distance of 156 miles (250 kilometers). It's unknown how people in antiquity moved them that far; water transport was used for part of the journey. Recently, scientists have raised the possibility that during the last ice age, glaciers carried these bluestones closer to the Stonehenge area and the monument's makers didn't have to move them all the way from Wales. So that may be one mystery solved. But what was the purpose of this combination of circular stones?

As Roseannadanna (Gilda Radner) used to say in her brash and tactless way, "It just goes to show you"—it just goes to show you what one can learn by listening to one's tour guide. Gilda, you remember, died early in her life of ovarian cancer. I think of this because of Donna's own genetic history. Gilda's husband, Gene Wilder, was a great comedian himself.

The purpose of Stonehenge's existence is another hotly debated issue, as records are so sparse from the time of its construction. It may have been used as a memorial to commemorate leaders of the nearby tribes, a site of miracle healing, a burial ground, or an astronomical observatory to mark the winter solstice. Whatever its purpose, it was built with a sophisticated understanding of mathematics and geometry, as it is aligned with the rising and setting of the sun. But as other similar structures seen in other areas of the world, did it point to something else?

Divinely revealed religions across the world point to a single omnipotent deity. Even traditional faiths and mythology seem to point to the worship of a single deity in their origins. However, we can also observe polytheistic traditions that seem to have evolved from an erosion of monotheism. Humankind's nature yearned for a powerful creator and found solace in deities created in their own minds. Even the Greeks intermingled with their gods, but there was one overpowering god. As people observed eclipses, comets, meteorites, and the deaths of loved ones, they sometimes related to these larger, more powerful elements. Some people before the time of Abraham had begun to worship the sun and stars as a great power. Archaeology has unearthed many ancient structures with alignments to celestial bodies and the strong notion that those people worshipped stars, the sun, and the moon. Examples also include the pyramids of Egypt and Mexico and other structures on all continents.

Most people today believe in aliens—from ancient visitors to modern-day extraterrestrials who visit earth with an agenda. Creation myths of each ancient civilization discuss alien gods who descended from the sky for any number of reasons, some of whom allegedly mated with human women to create bloodlines or created humans through biogenetic experiments. In the duality of physical reality, there would be good aliens and bad aliens, who would have great battles, just as we do while visiting here. The Sanskrit speaks of this.

As we search for the truth behind the illusion about who created humans and other sentient life forms, we look to those who came from the stars—ancient astronauts or creation gods.

One must never forget that if there are indeed extraterrestrials who are physical beings after a fashion, creation continues beyond their agendas. Call it a Grand Design, a Master Plan, or whatever term comes to mind. But remember, it had a beginning and is rapidly approaching its end, according to the Mayan calendar. Ancient alien theory grew out of the centuries-old idea that life exists on other planets and that humans and extraterrestrials have crossed paths before. This theme of human-alien interaction was prominent in the 1960s, driven by a wave of UFO sightings and popular films like *2001: A Space Odyssey* (1968). The NASA space program played no small part in this as well, and the question arose: if humankind could travel beyond our planet, why couldn't extraterrestrials visit earth?

So the question is did these structures point to our ancestral home whose alien visitors, recorded in many cultures, come to earth and in some way differentiate humans from beasts. I only say this because both Donna and I questioned many things about modern religion but wanted to believe in a single source of our being. If I today am to believe in angels and the soul, I would have to believe in a master planner or planners. Even in Genesis, the term *Elohim* refers to gods, not a singular god. Jacob and his ladder meeting with angels is as mystifying as Ezekiel's account in the Bible of several encounters with ancient astronauts in a shuttlecraft from another planet.

I remain unqualified to understand or uncover the sweet mysteries of life but am quite fascinated with this subject and how it relates to the soul. This will be covered later on in this story. In a more mundane fashion, I had fish and chips once more in my lifetime along with warm English ale. Donna did not eat anything; she looked quite tired, and in truth, our excursions on foot were very painful for her and limited to two blocks or so. A little pub was discovered by our cousins, and we slowly made it there. It broke my heart to see her so crippled, but the worst was yet to come.

The next part of our trip required us to travel to Paris. I remember traveling back and forth to England, and you recall that first time in the 1960s when I was in military service, flying in a small plane and losing my wedding ring. But we saw the white cliffs of Dover, as I whiteknuckled it across the channel. After that time and in later years, we came and arrived via Heathrow with larger planes supporting us above the clouds.

Today, if a trip including London and Paris is on your list, traveling by train through the Channel Tunnel (or the Chunnel as it's more commonly known) will likely be part of your journey. Although you have the option to take a ferry, fly, or even swim, the Eurostar train will whisk you between London and Paris under the English Channel. You may be surprised at the feat of engineering the tunnel truly is. The Channel Tunnel is a rail tunnel linking London and Paris beneath the English Channel at the Strait of Dover. At its lowest point, it is 250 feet deep and at 23.5 miles long. The tunnel has the longest undersea portion of any in the world. We booked it as it would be a new experience. It was fascinating. We sat across from each other as couples and were served a three-course meal and snacks if we wished. It ran from St. Pancras International Station in London under the English Channel to Gare du Nord in Paris. The train runs at high speed for most of the trip.

The Last Time I Saw Paris

Song composed by Jerome Kern, with lyrics by Oscar Hammerstein

The last time I saw Paris,
Her heart was young and gay.
No matter how they change her,
I'll remember her that way.

Yes, the last time we saw Paris, many years before, the song fit us in so many ways. We were young and gay, very much in love with this beautiful city. We did not bother with taxis; we used the underground to get anywhere we wished, traveling on both banks of the Seine River. We of course took the cruise tour on the Seine at night and saw all the famous sites. It was beautiful to see this city at night when it was all aglow. I think it has been called the City of Light, but it was also the city of enlightenment.

I remember a second visit later in the 1980s, when I was privileged to deliver a paper on a new medical advancement. I was given a commemorative bronze metal, which I used as a paperweight for many years. Unfortunately, this medal disappeared from my office because metal theft had started to accelerate and people were stealing scrap metal when the prices of it rose. This even happened on our family plot, where thieves ripped away the bronze plaques containing photos from the gravestone, threw away the pictures, and damaged the monuments. I used to fondly remember my parents and family by gazing at their photographs. When stolen, this was gone forever.

"Our Last Summer," Abba
I can still recall our last summer
I still see it all
Walks along the Seine, laughing in the rain
Our last summer memories that remain …

We were indeed to incorporate these memories into our latest visit, as this was probably to be our last major trip to Paris, but it was still exciting for us, nonetheless. The beguine had slowed immensely though. It was not at all like our previous visits to Europe. We had to take it by the day, not yet realizing that our worries were not far away. We walked hand in hand more than we ever did. Donna was still smiling through her pain, just happy to be with her cousins—even more so great, compatible friends. No, I had no premonition at this time, just a happiness that we were together and protectiveness more acute than I had ever experienced before. There was, of course, the regret that we were older and a fear of dying at our age, just as Donna earlier expressed in her life summary, which she divided into four quarters. Realizing that the alternative to aging could have been far worse, we carried on, slowly dancing through our life.

This time, it was quite different. We arrived in Paris after leaving the Chunnel. The railroad station was busy with travelers going in many directions to different destinations. There was an immediate change. There before us were young girls in long skirts, wandering around the station, and I would have to imagine up to no good. They were Gypsy girls, perhaps innocent, but the soldiers everywhere did not think so. Within moments, we noticed a fully armed soldier coming up to a young lady moving toward some travelers and asking her to leave. This, incidentally, is something we were going to see all over Paris, be it at the Louvre, the Eiffel Tower, any of the national museums and government buildings, and on all the streets. You see, we traveled at a time when major European cities were under attack by Islamic extremists. Every few minutes, we heard sirens going off and soon found that in this new threatened world, the Paris that was in our minds was no more. There was a certain tension in the air.

We found our prearranged taxi driver who said he would accommodate all four of us and our luggage. He said something in French and then hastily took off. As we exited the station, we were greeted by mobs of people and a polyglot of languages. I immediately had a biblical flashback to the Tower of Babel. Was it now located in Paris? You see, France, like England, was once a colonial power, and many people from all over the world left their poor countries and immigrated to the large cities of France, as well as all over Europe. I said, "S'il vous plait," to many people surrounding us, and basically, they kept carrying on with their conversations. I knew a smattering of French and was desperately trying to catch up with our driver. But there he was, lucky for us, around the corner packing our bags into his small cab. You see, Donna was never a light packer, so this was to be a huge challenge. We asked the driver if he knew where we were going, and as expected, his services had been arranged and he knew the hotel we were staying at. We arrived at this hotel, and it was in a beautiful location across from the Louvre and the Tuileries Garden. There was statue of Joan of Arc in front of the hotel, and when we entered, it was a beautiful lobby. We could see the Eiffel Tower from a distance. One could utter "C'est magnifique!" but not for long.

We arrived at the hotel with great expectations. We were given the keys and ascended to our rooms. Did I say room? It was more like a closet, with just enough space for a bed and a piece of furniture to put our clothing in. I must admit that the bathroom was luxurious, with a large bath and a shower within the bath. The only problem was that the side of the bathtub was as high as the corn in Kansas, or to be more appropriate to the country we were in, as the ramparts from *Les Miserables*. Indeed, it was a battle just to climb in, and each of us had to lend each other a helping hand. The lighting in the room didn't sparkle but sparked intermittently. Donna and I could never figure out the sequence of turning some lights on and others off. We just laughed it off, being too tired to cry. In truth, Donna was quite tired and not looking her best. We were enthralled with the lobby and spent much time there in the small cafés and restaurant. It was much easier to do so, you see. They say Paris is a city to walk through, but honestly, we couldn't do it. This again broke my heart but made me even closer to her, not only with compassion but with love. I held hands with her, not only to keep her from falling but because my heart and soul demanded it. I no longer wished to go anywhere where my dearest could not. Though the streets were both historic and ancient, perhaps where many famous people and those of other eras had walked, they were not appropriate for a challenged person. This was to be true also in the other areas we visited, where there were simply no disability accommodations as we have in the States. Much of our walking was within a two-block radius of our hotel, and that was okay with me. I still had "Ma" Donna with me.

We had picked a scary time to go to Europe. The fear was less in England, and all seemed serene with business as usual. Perhaps it is the strength and tradition of the English. So many have said, "There'll always be an England." Humphrey Bogart in Casablanca said the same about Paris. But our fear heightened as we heard frequent sirens and the warnings.

For background information, during the first half of the mid-twentieth century, the Muslim population in Europe was extremely small. By the year 2000, that population had swelled to more than fifteen million, including five million in France, four million in Germany, and two million in Britain. Substantial Muslim populations also inhabit Spain, Italy, the Netherlands, and Belgium. Today, Muslims constitute the continent's largest religious minority and Islam its fastest-growing faith. Many European cities are already one-quarter Muslim; in numerous cities, the majority of the under-eighteen population is Muslim, and Mohammed is the most popular name among boys. Thousands of mosques with large congregations now dot the European landscape in virtually every city. A recent study calculated that fully 25 percent of Europe's population will be Muslim by the year 2020. The scholar Bernard Lewis has predicted a Muslim majority on the continent by the end of the twenty-first century.

As I mentioned, during this time, immigration has increased the number of European Muslims. That could have been part of the mob scene outside of the rail station when we first arrived. Islamic newcomers from such far-flung places as North Africa, Egypt, Yemen, Syria, and Iraq were drawn to Europe by their hopes of attaining a better standard of living than they could realize in their own countries. Many others (extremists), however, were asked to relocate through the sermons and teachings of militant Islamist leaders and imams who urged Muslims to subjugate Europe (and America) by the sheer force of numbers. Large numbers of Muslim immigrants to Western Europe have sought to impose their fundamentalism on others, in order to create a new Islamic world (a caliphate, I believe it is called). Those fundamentalist Muslim immigrants and spokesmen pressured Western societies into supporting aspects of Sharia (Islamic Law) into the jurisprudence system, for example in England. France has been a little tougher, where women can't get a driver's license if their faces are covered.

Likewise, some have asked that the native cultures make concessions to Islamic traditions in the spirit of diversity. Yet Islamic immigrants do not assimilate easily into their host societies, often rejected as alien to the local culture. Others reject local rules and push for the creation of a (Muslim-only) state within a state. This is in contrast to a melting pot society. A new form of ghettoism has arisen in Europe where one has witnessed the rapid rise of exclusively Muslim neighborhoods, where few members of the native population or police officers are ever seen. What a shame not to share in the richness of different cultures. Paris, for example, is now surrounded by a ring of Muslim neighborhoods fitting this description. Many are young people, unemployed, and roaming the streets. Many of you have heard about the rash of fires, especially automobile burning.

Many of the issues with Western and Islamic problems also stem from European colonialism as well as a society where there are haves and have-nots. Note the recent term *the Arab Spring*. It is my belief that the Islamic religion is as noble as Christianity and Judaism but is being distorted by some who may be called militant. Let me give you an example from when we were in Paris.

When we arrived in August 2010, there were threats of a possible Mumbai-style terror attack on Western interests in Europe, which were considered credible. The thought was that al-Qaeda-linked organizations in northwest Pakistan had aim on targets in France, Germany, or the United Kingdom. They were going to attack multiple centers in Europe over a few days, said an official, who also spoke on condition of anonymity. "They are going to shoot the hell out of people and terrorize the entire country involved."

There were two bomb threats on the Eifel Tower when we were there, and we had made arrangements to have dinner there followed by a river cruise on the Seine. This was a bit unnerving. I tried to minimize it, not to get Donna upset. We just tried to live it day by day. Our government said not to give in to terrorism but to be cautious and aware of our surroundings.

Having experienced this and having lived a long time, I feel it's important to tell you that the conflicts then and now are not only about Islam, my friends. They are about people and radicalism and militancy. It is not only one religion against another (holy wars). There have been struggles within religions, within sects, and among people. We are on Mother Earth, not utopia. It is easy to influence disadvantaged young people. Look at the history in America alone to put this into proper perspective. When something triggers anger, the resulting protest is not always in an orderly fashion but rather turns to violence with people destroying property and attacking other people. This happened in America when Martin Luther King Jr. died. And I remember the

Chicago riots during the Democratic Convention. The primary cause of the demonstrations and the subsequent riots during the 1968 Chicago convention was opposition to the Vietnam War. Young peace activists had met at a camp in Lake Villa, Illinois, on March 23 to plan a protest march at the convention. The police were brutal with mace and billy clubs. A person Donna had dated many years before marrying me was attacked and ended up as a quadriplegic. So violence is part of all civilizations, and it continues to this very day and this very minute as I write this story.

Islam itself is a wonderful religion and way of life. It has contributed many great things to society, from poetry to mathematics, and had primarily lived in peace with all for centuries. For example, the alphabet is an Arabic name. The poet Omar Khayyam created a geometric to cubic equation, a feat that is regarded as "one of the most original discoveries in Islamic mathematics" (Wikipedia). The greatest contribution to the Ptolemaic planetary system (our understanding of the motion of the planets including our own) until the coming of Copernicus was made by the Persian Nasir al-Din al-Tusi from his work on spherical trigonometry.

Medicine is one area of science in which the Islamic world really excelled. Muslim doctors were far more advanced than those in the West for a time. Islamic medicine was practical and relied on observations and experiments. They also taught cleanliness to medieval Europe with hand-washing long before Semmelweis came on the scene and bacteria and other microbes were known to exist.

And all of us know the works of Khalil Gibran, whose words have helped me through my bereavement. Here is a small sample of what I mean.

"Ever has it been that love knows not its own depth until the hour of separation."

"The timeless in you is aware of life's timelessness. And knows that yesterday is but today's memory and tomorrow is today's dream."

You can see then what I mean about respect for the Islamic culture and most of the good and noble people. Donna and I had to learn a poem about Abu Ben Adhem and his dreams of peace in our early school years. This spoke about dreams of peace and a noble Muslim and was written by Leigh Hunt many years ago.

Donna would not have liked to see what is happening based on the radical elements within Islam. She would have feared for her children and grandchildren and all future generations.

Another group of people that are often misjudged are the Romani. The Romani people are of Indian origin, and we encountered them in Paris at the train station when we first arrived. The young girls in their swirling skirts did not seem so bad after all, just annoying. They too had been influenced by the scores of years wandering in caravans from country to country, never having one place to call home and many times subjected to genocide, sterilization, persecution, and excommunication from many lands. The Romani differ from other people because they have never identified themselves with a territory; they have no tradition of an ancient and distant homeland from which their ancestors migrated, nor do they claim the right to national sovereignty in any of the lands where they reside. Romani identity is bound up with the ideal of freedom of having no ties to a homeland. They too have been called outcasts or second-class citizens. The other rap from those whose culture they dwell in is that they are the kings of conniving, deception, trickery, stealing, and on occasion more serious crime. That is not true of the majority. It is always the minority that people point to. When Donna and I lived in our little town in Germany, there was a gypsy caravan quite close to us. Again, the majority are judged by the minority, and the majority of the Romani are not conniving thieves. They never harmed anyone. The romanticism reminded me of a favorite song of mine called "Golden Earrings."

"Golden Earrings" was written by Ray Evans, Jay Livingston, and Victor Young.

> There's a story the Gypsies know is true
> That when your love wears golden earrings
> She belongs to you ...

We had learned that in Paris, they considered Americans to be the best subjects upon which to ply their trade, so I resorted to a simple trick. Do you remember when President John Kennedy said, "Ich bin ein Berliner"? Having lived in Germany, my trick was not to respond in English (US variety), and if they were persistent or crowding in on Donna or me, I would say that I was German. "Ich bin Deutsch." And you know, they left us alone.

Traveling in a foreign country is always one of the most interesting parts of the adventure because it differs from traveling in one's own country. The four of us chanced to take a bus ride one day, and we had no idea where we were going. We had gone shopping in a remote area of the city and with no taxi cab hopped on the city buses, not being able to read the signs or converse with the bus driver. We tried to be nonchalant and oh so cool. Eventually, after a multidirectional trip, we got off and hailed a cab.

When we got in the cab, I forgot to ask our driver if he or she spoke English and that got us into trouble. We also did not know the address of our hotel or what street (*la rue*) it was on. As long as were with our tour guide, we had no trouble conversing, but none of us were well enough versed in French (Donna studied it in school). We knew a smattering of expressions like *bonjour, bon soir, au revior, merci,* and *oui.*

The cabdriver looked at us, and we looked at him, trying to tell him where we wanted to go. It was tough going for a while. I said, "American," and his face lit up. He asked what city, and I said Chicago. "Chicago," he said, and then he came up with Michael Jordan and the Chicago Bulls, immediately followed by Al Capone. I guess that era lives on in the minds of people in foreign lands who watch too many old-time movies or adore the mystique of the American gangster. Finally with this done, I think Susan said, "Take us to the Louvre." That worked, as the hotel was right across the street.

Another time, we hailed a cab to leave the Eiffel Tower, as Donna was not able to walk down to the riverbank for our nostalgic cruise. We bid our cousins good-bye. The very nice traditional Frenchman driving our cab did not understand a word we were saying. Then I remembered the key word. Take us to the Louvre. That he understood. Thank you, Susan and Elliot, for suggesting that we leave because it was too hard for Donna. But I claim the prize for getting us back to the hotel. If not, I could be an expatriate in France to this day. Boy, with all our foreign adventures, we could have landed up in any country.

During our visit, France was on red alert for a terrorist attack and had deployed thousands of police and soldiers to "sensitive" locations after at least four bomb threats at the Eiffel Tower and railway stations in the past two weeks about the time we arrived. On the night of our reservation for our full-course meal at the tower, it was opened. But the passage from our bus to the famous tower was crowded with all kinds of vendors. They were selling all kinds of souvenirs as they had done for years. This time, though, we were warned to watch our belongings and money carefully. The number of fully armed soldiers all around us was shocking. We had to wait for quite a while and had to go through a very careful bag and baggage search before being allowed to ascend to our dinner engagement.

You see, with Donna's arthritis and an agreement to eat in the local, less-expensive places and stay away from tourist traps, we spent much time eating crepes or other local dishes. We had treated ourselves to this extra special night out. Reading the brochure back home, it stated that one had to be spruced up. So the ladies in all their finery and Elliot and I with jacket and tie looked forward to a more formal evening out. You might find it interesting, but the young set in Paris were standing in line for hours to get into the Parisian version of McDonald's. The only other really nice restaurant in our neighborhood that we could walk to was a Chinese restaurant, of course.

We boarded the tour bus and then glanced around thinking we were on the wrong bus taking us to dinner. Wrong! We forgot how casual the world had become. The four of us stood out rather conspicuously in all our finery while the rest were in very casual clothing to say the least. At least the head waiter recognized the effort we had gone to and led us to a window table overlooking magnificent Parisian sites. Elliot and Susan had to ascend the stairway to the restaurant waiting for us, as Donna could not make the stairs. The restaurant was very accommodating though and took us up via the waiters' elevator and back down when we were finished. That's life, or as they say in France, "C'est la vie!"

I just had a sentimental thought as I am recording our memories through life.

You all remember *Fiddler on the Roof* and the song "Do You Love Me" sung by Tevye and Golda. In reverse, I have to profess that for fifty-seven years, I loved one woman with my heart and soul. This song was written by Jerry Bock and the lyrics by Sheldon Harnick. The memory of this just came to me, and it has to be part of the music and dance of our life. We were in a romantic city, and I was very sentimental about Donna in those days. I had no idea why other than our long journey together and my love for her. Was there, however, a premonition of things to be, somewhere deep within my subconscious? I cannot tell.

Anyway, Golda, in part of the song, says to Tevya:

> For twenty-five years I've lived with him
> Fought him, starved with him
> Twenty-five years my bed is his
> If that's not love, what is?

I say it doesn't change a thing. We lived as one for fifty-seven years, went through rough times and sweet times, fought a little, and cared enough to keep dancing to our beguine and to the music of our life. And though she is gone from me and this physical world, it does not change, alter, or destroy her presence. She remains in my heart, and I know that my beguine has ended, but as long as I believe in the soul, she is still part of my universe forever. Let me continue with a nice part of our trip to add continuity to this chapter.

As I said, it was our intent to see the Louvre and once again the famous art, such as *Venus de Milo* and Leonardo da Vinci's *Mona*

Lisa. There was also a new part of the entrance called the Louvre pyramid. It seemed so close, but when we started to walk, it was soon apparent Donna could not make it. The closer destination was the Tuileries Gardens, the extension of the Louvre. It was once a part of the extravagant area for French rulers but now was open to all citizens. We could see the Arc de Triomphe and the Eiffel Tower in the distance. The day was beautiful, and we sat on the benches just watching people and admiring the architectural pleasures. It was to me yet another day of serene pleasure just to be with my wife. I knew she was ill but not for the reasons to follow. Afterward, we did a little sightseeing within our expected and doable perimeters. Donna loved to shop, and there were stores and stands lining the streets leading to our hotel.

During our stay in France, we visited little villages, saw thatched roofs, and made the necessary stop at Versailles, the palace of Louis XIV. It was going to be an impossible task to visit this luxurious place. We were able to find an area where there were a few old wheelchairs. This made it easier inside, going from one elegant room to another, but once outside, we both had trouble walking down an area of slanting cobblestones.

However, we reached perhaps the most interesting sight to see, and Donna once again was energized: Claude Monet's garden, Giverny.

Much of this was so visual and so enchanting for both of us, especially since we had seen and admired his paintings in art institutes. I have to say that the ability to describe it in detail is beyond me. But it brought us both great joy. We again had difficulty traversing the place, so a custodian let Donna and me enter directly through large iron gates. I thought this would be optimal. I'll tell you in short order why it was a one-way ticket to paradise and a hell of a way for us to exit.

First, I must rely on the brochures I saved to describe this wonderland of beauty, color, and sheer magic. The land is divided into flowerbeds where flower clumps of different heights create volume. Fruit trees or ornamental trees dominate the climbing roses, the long-stemmed hollyhocks, and the colored banks of annuals. Monet mixed the simplest flowers (daisies and poppies) with the most rare varieties. Claude Monet did not like organized or constrained gardens. He married flowers according to their colors and left them to grow rather freely. This is precisely what my sweet artist Donna did with her needlepoint work. We noticed in the house volumes and volumes of books on botany and always looked for rare plants. The water garden was magnificent, and we learned that in 1893, ten years after his arrival at Giverny, Monet bought the piece of land neighboring his property on the other side of the railway. It was crossed by a small brook, a tiny tributary of the Seine River. The water garden was full of asymmetries and curves. It was inspired by the Japanese gardens that Monet knew from the prints he collected avidly. We saw the famous Japanese bridge covered with wisterias, other smaller bridges, weeping willows, a bamboo wood, and above all, the famous nympheas, which bloom all summer long. The pond and the surrounding vegetation form an enclosure separated from the surrounding countryside. Here is what separated Monet from other artists. Never before had a painter so shaped his subjects in nature before painting them. Always looking for mist and transparencies, Monet would dedicate himself less to flowers than to reflections in water, a kind of inverted world transfigured by the liquid element. I am sure many have seen copies of the Japanese garden series to which he devoted a great deal of his artistic career. I hope that some of you will have the pleasure of seeing it in person as we did.

As we left, we found that that large gate that let us in was locked. This then forced us to walk a long distance and then up a large number of stairs to exit. That was the hellish part I had mentioned.

This was the last of our tour except for a car tour of Paris and its lovely boulevards and parks. We even walked hand in hand down the famous Champs-Élysées and stopped for lunch. The street that was so quaint years ago was like any posh shopping center in the States with designer names and stores everywhere.

I bought some lovely trinkets and necklaces for Donna with the expectation that she would enjoy them when we got home. That was never to be. It matters not as the most precious jewel in my world was my Donna. Our life was soon to be torn asunder.

Chapter 24

• •

Back Home

Love and Devotion

Matt Monro was born Terry Parsons in north London in 1930, to Alice and Frederick. He had three brothers, Arthur, Reg, and Harry, and a sister, Alice. It was a tough childhood; his father died when he was three, and after his mother became ill, he was fostered out for two years. He was able to turn his pain into love songs. "Love and Devotion" is one that fits me to a T.

> My love will grow deeper as time passes by
> Deep as the ocean and as high as the sky
> My love, my devotion are yours till I die …

We had come home from Europe somewhere in early October 2010. We were back to our normal routine and reunited with Cheryl, Sara, Leah, and our friends. One Saturday morning, we went to a local pancake house for breakfast. After sitting there for a while, Donna said that she didn't feel well and wanted to go home. Once at home, she went right to bed, and I knew something was wrong. It was not an upset stomach or her advancing arthritis. I came into the bedroom when she started to complain about sharp chest pain. She was breathing with difficulty, was very pale, and had a very rapid pulse. Donna always hated to go to doctors or hospitals, but I convinced her that she must do so. Thankfully, I used my sense over my sensitivity when it came to my wife. We got to the emergency room and soon found out that she had a blood clot in her lung, commonly known to doctors as a pulmonary embolism. This is a life-threatening condition and has to be treated immediately. We mentioned to the doctors that we had recently been on an overseas trip and asked if this could be the reason. That could've been a logical explanation, but in time, we found it was not.

She was admitted and immediately started on blood thinners, at first administered through the skin of her abdomen and much later on, converted to oral medication. I, being a physician, was able to give her the medicine both orally and into her stomach. I imagine that it hurt, as I could see tears in her eyes. We had visiting nurses, who checked the level of her blood thinners regularly.

I must backtrack a bit and mention that Donna had been experiencing bouts of vomiting and a change in her bowel habits with bleeding from time to time. I had asked her to check this out, but with her distaste for tests and needles, she deferred doing so. Donna once told me when her dad, a family physician, was vaccinating the family, she ran into the bathroom and locked the door. That trick was not to work this time.

We saw her internist, who informed us that the cause was likely not due to the travel but more likely to an internal problem. As a physician, I realized that the doctor was putting two and two together and thinking of a cancer. I also knew that people with cancer often developed increased clotting of their blood, making them prone to a blood clot. A series of tests was set up in order to establish a diagnosis. Of course, Donna, knowing her family history, said, "It finally got me."

Loving You through It

"Gonna Love You through It," sung by Martina McBride and listened to by Donna, my lover of country-western music, is so appropriate for this next section of that which I variably call a memoir and a dance through life, specifically a serious change in the tempo of our life. I don't think Martina had breast cancer at the time she sang this but was raising awareness to it.

"Gonna Love You through It" is the title of a song written
by Ben Hayslip, Sonya Isaacs, and Jimmy Yeary

It is a beautiful song, and I can't print it all here. I urge you to get a copy of the words.

And when this road gets too long
I'll be the rock you lean on
Just take my hand, together we can do it
I'm gonna love you through it.

To paraphrase it, a woman's fear was confirmed that she had breast cancer, and her husband was there to comfort her while holding back his own tears as well as fears. He told her that he would be there for her and promised she would never be alone. Here are but a few of the words, and believe me, this was my sentiment and my role that I played during that long struggle.

From October 2010 to January 2011 she went through several tests, including a special one, which confirmed that she had a cancer in her colon. The specialist who did the final staging told us that it was a stage III or advanced disease. Our next steps were those of surgical consultation and cancer specialist consultation. I don't know how we took this all in. But I knew I had to do everything in my power to keep her spirits up, to support her, and to love her. I knew what was in her mind, but at that point, there were not any discussions, but rather, we took it day by day and moment by moment. After all, I had survived cancer a few years earlier, so I expected her to do the same. The doctors told us that she would have to go through radiation and chemotherapy before any surgery. So this was not immediately scheduled.

Our days from January 2011 to June 2011 on were spent with daily visits to the radiation expert and the cancer expert for office visits and chemotherapy and radiation therapy. I was with her on every trip to the hospital, and we now needed a wheelchair to make it easier for her. There was something different about my mood. It was more than regret, fear, or love. Again, there was something like a foreboding about losing a part of me. To that point, I had not crystallized my thoughts about the soul and what it is, and would do so, but I was reminded more about the case of identical twins who can perceive what is going on with their sibling when something is amiss. I was suffering and physically and emotionally going downhill with her. I had a foreboding that something was wrong and that in some way, a part of me was sick. She had fallen a few times, as I did. Her arthritis was bad, and I developed arthritis in my knees. She was short of breath, and my asthma returned. It seems when you love someone so much as in the case of cancer, it is not a solitary illness but affects the family.

Surgery was scheduled for June 10, 2011. We were told that this would be robotic surgery. It has become a popular method these days for all kinds of conditions. Robotic surgery is a method to perform surgery using very small tools attached to a robotic arm. The surgeon controls the robotic arm with a computer. Robotic surgery is similar to laparoscopic surgery. It can be performed through smaller cuts than open surgery. The small, precise movements that are possible with this type of surgery give it some advantages over standard techniques. We agreed to the procedure because benefits include:

- faster recovery

- less pain and bleeding

- less risk of infection

- shorter hospital stay

- smaller scars

And when that day came, my daughter and Donna's friend were there to support Donna and of course knowing my anxiety, me as well. It was a lengthy procedure, and it seemed Donna was resigned and calm. But I knew her fear, and there was the same visceral fear within me.

The surgeon came out many hours later and told us that all went well and that she was stable but needed several hours in recovery. She was then transferred to a surgical bed. In addition, in order to rest the remaining part of the colon, she had an ileostomy performed. An ileostomy is a surgical procedure in which the small intestine is attached to the abdominal wall in order to bypass the large intestine; digestive waste then exits the body through an artificial opening called a stoma (from the Greek word for "mouth"). This was to be a temporary one, as the doctor felt it would be reversed in time when her own colon regained some function. We were referred to an ileostomy nurse for training, as the bag could leak or become obstructed and the entire apparatus that connected to the body had to be changed every five days or so, or sooner if a complication arose. Donna hated the tight stocking she had to wear and the pain that she always feared, and she could not look at this apparatus, as she always had a certain distortion of her self-image. She was immaculate in every way. I have to bless the agile mind of my daughter, who caught on to the process and was the only person who could regularly change the bag or all of its component parts. May life never impose this on her. I have so much love and gratitude for her, and she once told me that she did not move on with her life, knowing that she would somehow be needed.

The surgeon, in addition to removing a good part of the colon, also removed the chain of nodes adjacent to the colon and deeply seeded in the abdomen. He told Donna and me that twenty-four out of twenty-four lymph nodes were free of malignancy and the colon cancer that had been of a serious stage (III, as you recall) was now stage I. I was thankful and tried my best to cheer her up. She had a heavy load hanging over her with that horrendous family history. Even one of her closest cousins had died of lymphoma, so it was striking the next generations, her generation and soon her two nieces.

We came home surrounded by our little family and supported by home health nursing. Basically, Murphy's law states that anything that can possibly go wrong does, and it did. I can't remember the sequence of things that went wrong, but there were many:

1) falling frequently

2) dehydration

3) urinary tract infection

4) continued loss of weight, at one point down to a hundred pounds with muscle wasting

5) the development of fever and a fistula (opening) from her colon deep into the pelvis, which required a drainage tube to be inserted and then six weeks of intravenous antibiotic treatment that had to be administered in a local rehabilitation center

6) during trips back to the hospital, I noticed her inability to know where she was only to find that her brain had atrophied

7) continued decrease in awareness of her surroundings and interest in food she always liked. She specifically enjoyed a toasted cheese sandwich, remarking that no one could make this sandwich better than her loving daughter.

At night, we shared our bed of fifty-seven years and would watch some of her favorite television programs. I held her hand, cuddled with her, and serenaded her with my poor voice but excellent piano playing. I could not give up, could not let her go, and continued to reassure her that all would be well. Again, it was out of love, comingled with my fear and that nebulous thing I keep talking about, my soul mate.

I encouraged her to try to have the fistula closed, but Murphy's law prevailed. There were several attempts to try to pack it and suture it, but the surgeon told us that her colon (probably from the radiation) was like parchment and would not take the sutures to close it. The last attempt led to massive bleeding from a large deep vein in her body, and that was the end of it.

At last, I convinced Donna that we needed help and so we contacted a home health agency, requesting initial daytime help so that I could work a few hours a day (not that I cared but we needed some income to help with the bills). This soon graduated to around-the-clock gals, who were all compassionate, all kind, and most important, relieved my poor daughter from the nightly draining of the ileostomy. Donna protested quite a bit but did give in. When the night crew came on initially, I still stayed in our bedroom. After a while, my panic attacks and sheer exhaustion set in, and I had to sleep in the den. At the same time, the corporation I was working for connected me with my office through a remote system. This way, I could be home with my loved one at all times. These girls often said that I was the most devoted husband they had ever encountered. They too could not understand that special attachment we had and observed me with my soul mate.

As long as I had Donna, our beguine and our dance of life continued but in a very slow tempo. From my musical training, I can tell you that a very fast tempo, prestissimo, has between 200 and 208 beats per minute, presto has 168 to 200 beats per minute, allegro has between 120 and 168 beats per minute, moderato has 108 to 120 beats per minute, andante has 76 to 108, adagio has 66 to 76, larghetto has 60 to 66, and largo, the slowest tempo, has 40 to 60. We were largo, a far cry from our younger days and the tumultuous periods of our life. Largo means slow and stately, and up to the bitter end, she was a person of substance and always stately.

Donna's high school had a sixty-year reunion for the class of 1952, held June 16, 2012. Yes, we went with much difficulty, using her caregivers and a wheelchair. She needed to be there, as sick as she was, and people flocked around her. She seemed quite stoic and a bit silent and did not eat very much, nor did we stay very long. She was happy to reunite with so many pals and was thrilled when a Hollywood producer and writer by the name of Joe Siegman came up to her. Many of her classmates were very successful; one gentleman was now a Georgia state legislator. Her closest friends flocked around her all evening. The sad part for me was that she was the only person at the reunion who was in a wheelchair. I can still picture the photographs they took with Donna in the center, up front. Well, that is fitting, as she was the center and core of my life.

As I had time to reflect on our road that we had traveled, I thought of the song "Young Love." But to me, in the now of each moment of her illness, I thought to myself, *The body ages, but love does not!* You see the words *young love* and *first love*, filled with sheer devotion, which goes on to say deep emotion. You see, she was my one and only, and the devotion mixed with emotion were still at work. So not only in the young days but in the "golden years," love is always strong. At least, ours was.

Donna's cousin Stu came to visit and presented her with a video made from tapes from their childhood days. We watched the video, and there was little Donna with her big smile visiting Riverview with her parents. Perhaps we were there at the same time. Who knows if this was the earliest melding of our souls, and of course as young kids, we could not know each other. Was it nothing more than us having a good time? I now wonder of I may have been on the same ride with her or at the same ice cream parlor or vendor.

This is the most difficult chapter of our life to recall and to tell. There was no humor in it. Donna went through the various stages of dying, and I went through the various stages of mourning. I know she wanted to live, but in the end, she kept saying, "I can't take this anymore," and she was jumpy, nervous, and thrashing about. We had to call in hospice services at home. When medical care cannot offer a cure, hospice provides care, comfort, and support for persons with life-limiting conditions, as well as their families. That was the situation we were in. One day, the hospice nurse said she needed to be transferred to their facility, and it was out of my control. She had become much more nervous, and incoherent; she was begging to be sedated and thrashing about, and the professionals said this was the time. I sat there numbly, watching them taking her away from me forever.

The morning or so after she was admitted—and they did everything to keep her comfortable—I had a sudden feeling of urgency and a fear came over me. And so at a very early hour, I rushed to her room. There was my Donna; she was breathing very slowly from the drug cocktail they had given her. I could not bring myself to tell her it was all right to go. Instead, I kissed her lips tenderly. She took two more breaths, and then she was gone. I still did not want to let go. I tried to breathe my life into her but to no avail.

The Lost Soul

In the still of a holiday night
Past, present and that yet unknown
Thought merges together in the depth within me

Life's sadness carried within
Often now as broken glass
Each splinter reaching
A tired and broken heart

Yet within my mind exists
Those sweeter memories
They soothe and still
The restless soul within me resides

The comfort of our younger days
A parent's love, wife's devotion
Scents of celebration, carefree days
And yes the days of loss
But always shared together

When warmed by those days
My table ran over with love
The shards of sorrow and the bittersweet
Are dispelled by sweet memory

She was the jewel that would shine
Within my very being
She was there to strengthen and enfold

She was my warming light
That captured my soul with her love

Perhaps, I can some day
Rekindle that light
And find a soothing path
But for now it's sweet memory
My soul does weep
It is torn in two
It functions yet, but suffers much
As it searches deeply for that which it lost

I wish for a sign to light the way
To dance the dance of life alone
The path of life traversed alone
My love for her must strengthen me
To go on.

Chapter 25

$\bullet \quad \bullet$

After the Dance Is Over

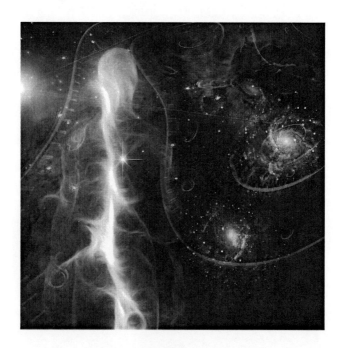

Or Is It?

Is That All There Is?

Wandering aimlessly after her death, I happened upon Thomas Moore's "'Tis the Last Rose of Summer," and I thought of my dear, dear Donna as my last love, as in this beautiful saying. Let me incorporate a portion of it here and now.

> When true hearts lie withered
> And fine ones are flown,
> Oh, who inhabit
> This bleak world alone?

This truly reflects how I felt at that moment of loss. She was my shining gem, and the world seemed bleak. Many tell me I was in a state of shock. Donna died May 11, 2013, right before Mother's Day. I remember little about the funeral and the mourning period that followed. I really had no solace from the visitation to our home during what in Judaism is called Shiva. After a Jewish funeral takes place, the immediate family (i.e., spouse, parents, children, and siblings) are considered the mourners. The immediate family begins "sitting shiva." *Shiva* means seven and is a seven-day mourning period that is observed. Let me tell you seven days was not enough and will never be enough for me.

During Donna's funeral, I was not able to deliver any words of meaning, being in a state of shock or emotional paralysis, but my grandchild, Sara, came up with the most beautiful sentiment. She said, "I will never hear, 'How are you, sweet girl?' or 'How are you, babes?' ever again. Maybe only in my head and heart but never in real life. Today, my life turned in a completely different direction, and I will never feel the same. I lost my best friend, my buddy who would I stay up watching movies till 2:00 a.m. with, and my second mother, who was there to raise me and who held me right after I was born, whose lap I sat on, whose shoulder I cried on, and who brushed my hair and rubbed my back until her arm felt sore. Today, I lost my bubbe (my grandma), who had lived with me since July 12, 1997, the day I was born. I love you so much, Bubbe, and nothing will ever change that. I know you're here to look down on me, and I will always try to make my Bubbles proud. Love you so much, Bub!"

Donna's death changed everything for me, and it sent me on a quest for answers in many areas of life. Music speaks to this for me, and I've shared some of these thoughts here. Perhaps the thoughts that spring forth from my very soul will lighten this section. It is difficult but to quote C.S. Lewis, "When I lay my questions before God, I get no answer." But I know that asking for help through prayer or petition is not enough. It is taking the time to listen, as you may discover God in the depths of your own heart. Thus, this is what I pour out for you right now.

Now that Donna has died, the music has stopped. The orchestra has left the bandstand of my life, and my dance with her has ended. My circle of family and friends has been shrinking, but the worst of all for me has been the death of my wife. I sit in quietude, often discontent, often in self-imposed exile from life.

My singular purpose of this chapter is a need to explore this relationship with Donna, whom I have called my soul mate. Is it all over? What does her death mean, and what is our connection, though one of us is now on a different journey. That reminds me, ever the musician, of the song "Loch Lomond." Loch Lomond is a famous location in Scotland for many reasons but one of them is definitely to do with a song, a poignant anthem of loss and sadness that is known throughout the world. This song seems to have meaning for people who have never been to Loch Lomond. But what is the real meaning and origin of this song, so popular on the world stage? The subject matter of the verses is tragic, dealing with loss and yearning. That is how I look at these words. I can't discover the composer, as that knowledge may be lost in antiquity.

> Oh you'll take the high road and I'll take the low road,
> An' I'll be in Scotland before you;
> But me and my true love will never meet again
> On the bonnie, bonnie banks O' Loch Lomond.

The bonnie, bonnie banks of my life were the days of our life together, and on this plain of existence, we shall never meet again. But is there to be another meeting in store? Let's try to explore this together.

I had hoped that Donna would come to me in a dream to reassure me, but I only had a dream the first day after the funeral. We, in the dream, were in a shopping center, and I left her for a moment, asking her to wait for me. When I returned, she was no longer there. I tried many ways to get to her, but all was to no avail. This dream of losing my way and not being able to get back to my home or a loved one has been recurrent in my life. I could never figure it out. But this time, it was as a nightmare. I felt hopeless and felt a part of me was torn away. Many have had a dream about their beloved spouse coming to them in a dream, smiling at them with reassurance that everything was all right. Is that what our mind seeks, or is there something more to it?

That is why my question remains, as in the Richie Valens song, "Donna, where are you?" The problem with her death is her total absence. I visit her grave site but know these are only earthly remains. I look at her photographs and that ever present smile, and it makes me sad. I look at her beautiful artwork, and I think of its beauty, yes, but what will happen to these works one day when I have left this world?

Being in a profound state of shock when Donna died, I was an empty shell and could not express my feelings in front of others. My dear granddaughter did so with great passion for her grandmother.

I loved Donna truly during our life together and felt that much of what we had to share would fade away as we stemmed our tide together. I now feel, with the new knowledge gleaned, she is near, as close as my heart, as close as my soul, and ever in my mind.

I recall a poem Donna used to recite. It was her favorite thought from her mother's book of sayings and poems. She used it a lot. Today, I need her strength and can, within my mind, still hear her voice as she recited it.

> After a while, you learn.
> The subtle difference.
> Between holding a hand.
> And chaining a soul.

Chapter 26

* *

You'll Never Walk Alone

Walk on, through the wind

Walk on, through the rain

Though your dreams be tossed and blown

Walk on, walk on, with hope in your heart

—R. Rodgers, O. Hammerstein

I have a comment about the song. It is one of the most inspirational works of music I have encountered and the tremendous talent of the composers speaks for itself.

Whether this memoir is merely to be a heritage offering and a remembrance for our many friends or I find a willing audience for my work of love is unknown. But I remain undaunted and convinced that this is a lasting eulogy for the one I loved and can touch so many others who have similar stories. If I bring them a measure of peace through my writings, I remain grateful that they chose to read the story of the road Donna and I traveled, and for all our loved ones, this is a reminder of their mom and pop and Donna and Joel Levin.

It is time to bring a little levity back, and so I shall! After Donna died in 2013, my own aches and pains intensified, specifically my left knee from an injury and my right hip, which had been destroyed by the yearly use of cortisone for my asthma. I found that the pain was getting bad, and worst of all, I could not walk my doggie.

The Humor

First off, I could not walk alone but was introduced to a cane or walking stick, something I had collected as a hobby. So it was my cane and me.

Secondly, I could not master curbstones, so my daughter, granddaughter, or whoever I was with had to lend a helping hand.

Then in February 2014, I had my hip replaced. From that time on, I could not walk alone. First, I walked with the help of the hospital therapist into the rehabilitation hospital, where for the most part, my new companions were the entire staff, including aides and therapists. I regressed from a cane to a walker. The next step was home therapy with physical and occupational therapy and finally weeks of outpatient therapy with a grand group of people. They even supplied me with a few corny but cute jokes. Let me try them on you:

Joel asks: What is a pirate's favorite restaurant?

You give up.

Joel says: It is Aarg-bies (Arby's)!

Joel asks: Why does a chicken coop only have two doors instead of four doors?

You giving up? Because if it had four doors, it would not be a coop but a sedan!

Anyhow, I am in recovery from the hip, but each day, I have a new twist. The businessman says, every day a new dollar. I have to say, every day a new dolor (meaning pain).

I am fortunate to have my daughter and granddaughter (and my pooch Leah) living with me. I wonder how fortunate they are with yet another burden for Cheryl and unsettlement in the mind of a young teenager. It seems that Sara finds escape when and where she can, and I can't blame her. I am a nervous man with that old black magic called separation anxiety as well as parental traits handed down to me by my family. In its duality, it can have a crippling effect on those I love.

My daughter takes me everywhere, and at this point in my life, I am on the receiving end of medicine and care rather than the giving end. I have had many appointments with a myriad of physicians, and Cheryl is always there for me. People don't realize how deep Cheryl is or how smart. Right now, she is reading a book, *Taking the Quantum Leap*, written by Fred Alan Wolf. How apropos considering she does not know I am pursuing the same quest in this memoir. Now my young driver, Sara, using her grandmother's car, ferries me around. Of course, it brings back my anxiety for her safety, and the separation thing I have plays a big part.

I also have recently started to get out with my good friends, Carol and Vern and Fred and Sheila. Cousins David, Bette, and Bob are there for me as well, so I shant have to walk alone. Lastly, my wife is always in my mind, resting in the bosom of my heart and depth of my soul.

They say that the caregiver of a loved one is often as sick as the ill, be it physically or mentally. By now, those of you within my life circle and those of you who have read this book must recognize my love of music. I was able to play the piano up to the day my wife died. And that is the day that my music ended. I can't manipulate my fingers on the keyboard, although I use a computer every day. It reminds me of my mother, who was an excellent artist; the day my father died, she never painted again. No one can figure it out, and perhaps it is psychological. The doctors say my hands are strong. It remains an unsolved mystery for me. Mind over matter in a negative sense.

In summary, I know that I am not alone, thanks to my support system, and the beautiful song that gave name to this chapter rings soundly in the circles of my mind. I still am in the darkness of grief and reluctant to walk on with that hope in my heart. I hope that it may yet happen.

That Lonesome Road

Nathaniel Shilkret was the composer and the lyrics were written by Gene Austin for the song "The Lonesome Road." I liked the Frank Sinatra version.

> Look up, look down that lonesome road
> Hang down your little head and cry, my love
> Hang down your little head and cry
> The best of friends must part some time
> And why not you and I my love

A number of years ago, I came upon this tremendous book, *The Road Less Traveled and Beyond: Spiritual Growth in an Age of Anxiety*[1] by M. Scott Peck, MD. It has much more meaning for me now, having experienced a myriad of problems. Dr. Peck is a psychiatrist, unlike the modern-day specialist who substitutes chemical cures for person-to-person interaction, in your eye and mind care, so to speak. There is a statistic that today's doctors spend less than twelve minutes with a patient. Most of that time is gazing at a computer screen. That does not leave time for discussion of problems or confronting them, be they physical, emotional, or spiritual, where my current quest lies.

The book was developed from Dr. Peck's lectures, which he has expanded and transformed into a unified and compelling presentation of his ideas and insights. Dr. Peck addresses urgent questions of personal and spiritual growth, including blame and forgiveness, the issue of death and meaning, self-love versus self-esteem, and sexuality and spirituality (all so essential for me). The book takes us from the first step in the spiritual journey, "Growing Up," to the next step, "Knowing Yourself," to the ultimate step, "In Search of a Personal God." As an agnostic, it is amazing to me how so many scientists believe in a creator. Take Einstein, for example, whom Dawkins called an atheist. Einstein made repeated references to "a superior spirit," "a superior mind," "a spirit vastly superior to men," "veneration for this force," etc. This is not atheism. It is clear Einstein believed that there is something beyond the natural, physical world—a supernatural creative intelligence. Further confirmation that Einstein believed in a transcendent God comes from his conversations with his friends. David Ben-Gurion, the former prime minister of Israel, records Einstein saying, "There must be something behind the energy. And the distinguished physicist Max Born commented, "He

---

[1]   New York: Simon & Schuster, 1997.

did not think religious belief a sign of stupidity, not unbelief a sign of intelligence." Therefore by Dawkins's own definition, Einstein is not an atheist. On one point, however, Dawkins is correct: Einstein did not believe in a personal God, who answers prayers and interferes in the universe. But he did believe in an intelligent mind or spirit, which created the universe with its immutable laws. That is a place that I am now moving to from an agnostic position, thanks to all I have read and all I feel, plus that emotional clinging of mine to the concept of the soul and my soul mate, who traveled with me through this lifetime.

Going back to Dr. Peck's inspirational book, reading it was a journey of self-discovery as well as an enlightening examination of the complexities of my life and my confused nature of belief.

Confronting and solving problems is a painful process, which I always tried to avoid. This avoidance resulted in a lot of pain and the hampered ability for me and my kids to grow both mentally and spiritually. Drawing heavily on his own professional psychiatric experience, Peck suggested ways in which confronting and resolving our problems and suffering through the changes can enable us to reach a higher level of self-understanding. He also discussed the nature of loving relationships: how to recognize true compatibility, how to distinguish dependency from love, how to become one's own person, how to be a more sensitive parent. I often wondered if I was much too dependent on Donna to make everything right. But I never doubted my love.

This book was developed from Dr. Peck's lectures, which he has expanded, coedited, and transformed into a unified and compelling presentation of his ideas and insights. With a rare combination of profound psychological insight and deep spirituality, Dr. Peck talks about the choices we make every day in business and at home and the ethical choices that may affect all of humankind. Dr. Peck addresses the differences between good and evil, the means of overcoming narcissism, loving and being loved, living with paradox, accepting the consequences of our actions all through life, and coming to terms with dying and death. Dr. Peck talked about the choices we make every day in business and at home and the ethical choices that may affect all of humankind. Dr. Peck's comments on overcoming narcissism speak to my prodigal son, who when I was critically ill once asked his mom in all seriousness, "What will become of me?" (referring to himself).

The following is a quote from his book:

> We have all come into one world and, undoubtedly from one source, on a single conscious journey to one's destination, a destination unknown to us all. A destination many believers on the subject of the afterlife claim to perceive. A destination almost all of us wish could be paradise. For many it's all about money and fame. The beginning of our consciousness/Awareness, that is our life, seems to be in this physical and transient world, subject to space and time and illusion. Yet our consciousness deep within us (the subconscious) conveys a message that we are nonphysical as well and immortal in part, which contradicts the reality of our transient physical life on earth. Religion and science as well as our self come to this conclusion in different ways, religion with its belief of life after death, science through the concept that matter can't die and we through our dreams, illusions and experiences such as recall of past lives, or near death experience.

This is the critical step in this our memoir. For the casual reader, it will have some meaning spiritually. As to the heritage worth of this book, the writing of it has created a method of projecting my personal thoughts onto my immediate family. To my friends who have walked with Donna and me along the road we mutually shared, I send my everlasting love. To my soul mate, it is too late to physically communicate with her but through my heart and with all my soul I have dedicated this memoir to memorialize and capture our life's journey.

Chapter 27

. . . .

Final words:
Notes to Family and Friends

I have written this book for many reasons. It was to memorialize my wife foremost. Second, it was to capture within my yet active and alert mind for you, the reader, all I remember about our life together— thus a memoir. Next, it is to remind those who walk with me, as I am not alone, of my gratitude to them. I wish to acknowledge them. And lastly, since this has been a wonderful outlet for my emotions, it is an attempt at recovery.

Much of what we had to share would fade away as we stemmed our tide together. I now feel that with the new knowledge gleaned, she is near, as close as my heart, as close as my soul. I mentioned much earlier that Jarlath Street was the site of our real home, but I had lived in this house with Donna for almost seventeen years. And a house without a mother, as well as a wife, is not a home at all. However, make no mistake, our home fires keep burning, thanks to Cheryl, my daughter, and I will include a few personal words for her. I also love my son Ken, who although miles away is in my heart right

249

now. I will also speak of him in these final thoughts. As to the son who left us so many years ago, I have not fully recovered from that and will have to have another speak the words of forgiveness that I can't as yet.

A Recovery Prayer

I've learned so much so in problems hold.
There's gain from pain, that's what I'm told.
I talked to God, some call it pray.
But listened not to what he'd say
It then seemed rigid, with no leeway
For now, for my own very being
This memoir seemed release to bring

The classic words I do respect
Of every religion and every sect
I do not judge, nor e'er demean
The way you think, the things you glean

There are similar quests not mine alone
We share in life, it's what we own
So hope the golden path we'll sight
To find the road, to see the light

I pray for clear mind, and not to hurry
Please let me relax, please let me not worry
I pray to keep ego out of the way
In things I do, and in things I say

Please teach me compassion show me resolve
Grant that I let go and let things evolve
But mostly I hope that the science I read
Will give me new hope, and plant a clear seed.

I think you know what I am about
To no longer fear, to no longer doubt
That heaven exists for a soul to abide
With angels and helpers to stand by her side.

And some day, for me, when my dance will be
through
With no words within me, when my life is through
My soul will survive beyond all mortal strife
And lead me to her, my soul mate, my wife.

My dad used to croon a tune to my mom. I think it was called "I
Love You Truly." It went like this and was written by Carrie Jacobs-Bond.

I love you truly, truly, dear.
Life with its sorrow, life with its tear,
fades into dreams when I feel you are near,
for I love you truly, truly, dear.

I loved her truly during our life together and ever in my mind.

Donna's death inspired me to think about many things, but mostly,
I think about what is left behind. What is it that we leave behind when
life is at its end? I don't mean materialistic things, such as inheritance,
possessions, or things you owned and things you loved. By the way,
you leave an awful lot of paperwork to be handled. I know what Cheryl

and I have gone through this past year. I am talking about a different legacy. It speaks to having lived life honestly and leaving behind a good name. My mother and my Donna were adorned with the crown of a good name.

And so, I also leave you with my love, my understanding, and my compassion, and I hope you will shed those devastating traits that I carry—worry, separation anxiety, and a lot of tears. Those you can do without!

This reminded me of the Irving Berlin song, and so once more this lover of music has adapted this to our children.

I'll be loving you always
With a love that's true always
When the things you've planned
Need a helping hand
I will understand always
Always
Days may not be fair always
That's when I'll be there always
Not for just an hour
Not for just a day
Not for just a year
But always …

I want you to know I will understand always. I know that life does not go on forever, and I won't always be here, but if you keep me in your heart, that can be as always. Don't forget your mom, dad, and grandparents, who loved you from the start.

For a Good Daughter

You know how silent I can be
Words today are hard for me
You try so hard to make it right
But sometimes it's a worthless fight

But remember your value, remember your worth
You've been my best treasure upon this old earth

I know, my child, when things went wrong
You tried your best, to get along
But that was then, and this is now
Forget the past, please take that vow

And remember your value, remember your worth
You've been my best treasure upon this old earth

Each day I ponder while trying my best
To let you know and let your mind rest
That your goodness shines forth, yes others must know
Your compassion came forth, when we were so low

But remember your value, remember your worth
You've been my best treasure upon this old earth

Some think they're better, some think they're wise
Pretense and ego, it's really all lies
In truth, child, from the time of your birth
Others knew naught of my child's true worth

Please remember your value, remember your worth
You've been our best treasure upon this old earth

I must tell you now, before I too rest
You did it all, you passed every test
If others but knew what I have known
That you have depth, and a goodness well shown

Please remember your value, remember your worth
You've been my best treasure upon this old earth

Your mom was sick for a very long spell
You stood by her; you did it so well
You rose to each task; you had such insight
Whether in morning or late in the night

You cared for your mother and always just right
Supported your Father with each crisis and fright
You as my child and me as a your dad
Reality hit us, and made us both sad

Please remember your value, remember your worth
You've been our best treasure upon this old earth

You did it all, with commitment and quest
Always with meaning, doing your best
I thank you for Mom; I thank you for me
You've been the good daughter that others can't see

Once more reminding, remember your worth
You've been our best treasure upon this old earth

I thank you for Mom; I thank you for me
You're at it again, now caring for me
I say this with gratitude; I give it much thought
You are the treasure that we always sought

A lasting emotion, remember your worth
You've been our best treasure upon this old earth

In ending these thoughts for all folks to know
Some rise to the challenge when things seem so low
There's nary a daughter on earth who can be
The kind of daughter you've meant to me

In ever reminding remember your worth
You've been our best treasure upon this old earth.

Thank you, my child!

For a Good Son:

Ken was always a cuddler when he was young. He would crawl into bed with his mom and his pop (that's what he calls me). Even this Father's Day, he thought nothing of finding his way into my bedroom to lie there and chat. He has always been a hard worker and has had some hard times. He loves the outdoors and works as an artisan when decorating people's pools. I am proud of the work that he does. Everybody can't be a doctor or lawyer. Remember, if I had to do it again, I would have remained in my musical career. And so I say:

My son, my son, listen to me
Be the person you're meant to be
Look for the good in all that you do
Have pride in yourself to see it through

You're at a distance, but far though that be
You're as close as the heartbeat in me

No person is bad or wholly is good
It's something to know and well understood
We all are but human, with much frailty
But I see so much good in your loyalty

You are at a distance, but far though you be
You're as close as the heartbeat in me

Your heart is quite open, you surely have shown
You adopted a family and called it your own
This deed makes me happy; it gives me some cheer
You'll never be lonely, with kind folks real near

You are at a distance, but far though you be
You're as close as the heartbeat in me

I speak to a good soul and tell everyone
The pride and the privilege to call you my son

Both you and your sister, how well I have known
I have these two gifts, no other can own

Remember, dear Son, though far you might be
You're as close as the heartbeat in me.

Thank you, Son.

To the Prodigal Son

I told myself from the start that this had to be an honest memoir,
no frills and no lies. I had to say what must be said. It's been so long
since I last saw him. When he left, he broke his ties with us and it
seems like forever. His mom is gone and left this earth as unhappy
and as sad as I am today. I am too emotional and bewildered about
this so I have to borrow the words of another. They are words that
touch my aching heart and come from that inspirational book that
my mother-in-law left for her daughter. In my earlier days, I paid it
little attention. Today, it is like a book of life, a book of humankind,
a remembrance that we are all in this together. Thank you, Rachel.
You've come to my rescue. The author I speak of is one named Edgar
Guest. It is called *If I Were Sending My Boy Away*. I never sent him
away, dear readers. He chose to go, and alas, I'll never know why.
My friend Vern knows how hard I tried to counsel and caution him
in every way.

He may never read this story or come across it, but he once was a
son we loved, our firstborn who wandered a bit too far from the apple
tree.

Here goes then with but a few of the magnificent words of Edgar Guest, who expressed so well what I cannot yet say in my heart for this lost son. The last stanza ends with:

> Trust me, wherever you chance to be
> No, there's nothing to hide from me
> Tell me it all—Your tale of woe
> That sting of failure that hurts you so …

I wish he could have talked to me. I was there to listen and try to help him figure out his problems. So, coming back to his mother and father was not to be, and it is now seventeen years later. Lastly, I hope that my son is alive. Yes, I tried to trace him, but the trail ended. Dear readers, losing a loved one to death is hard. Losing a live child is beyond any rhyme or reason. Fare thee well, Ray, and as I told the others, hold your head high.

To Our One and Only

My granddaughter lived with us from the time she presented herself to the world up to now when she has expanded her world. She will be a senior in high school this fall, and she is very much grown up. Her father moved to Chicago, and she had to establish a new relationship. He rarely came in to see her in her early years. Raising Sara was a joy, doing it all alone. But when he came back to the Midwest, things changed. Things will never change for me, as she is like a child to me, God giving me another chance. But habits don't change overnight, and I plead my case that it is a grandparent's prerogative to give of your all to your one and only. It's uncanny that she shows some traits of her great-grandmother, twirling her hair until she developed a bald spot, and many traits of her grandmother, whom she loved to call Bubbles. She loves clothing and all the accessories that go with it. She uses that which I call war paint, over her eyes, under her eyes, and on her lips and loves to have her nails done. She can, as they say, shop until she drops. One thing she loves from her mom is to be touched and given a special massage that my daughter is famous for. Cheryl's mom and dad were able to partake in this pleasure from time to time. So here are my thoughts.

To know that you're near
Always close to my heart
You were raised with us here
Right from the start
And so with much pride, I proudly exclaim
Remember, dear Sara, you carry our name

We taught you self-worth
I think we did well
We watched you mature
Our hearts they did swell

And so with much pride, I proudly exclaim
Remember, dear Sara, you carry our name

But ere I forget
Ere my tears start to smart
Your grandpa does know
Someday you will part

And yet with much pride, I proudly exclaim
Remember, dear Sara, you carry our name

We've had so much fun,
Your Bubbie and me
Having you here
Was our blessing you see

And yet with much pride, I proudly exclaim
Remember, dear Sara, you carry our name

You must know, my dear,
From the very first start
You've been fiber and core
Of your grandparents' heart

And so with much pride, I proudly exclaim
Remember, dear Sara, you carry our name

I also must warn you
That folks can bring blame
To you, my dear child
who carries our name

And yet with much pride, I proudly exclaim
Remember, dear Sara, you carry our name

I give some counsel
And words that are wise
There are folks that you'll meet
In devil's disguise

And so heed this warning I hereby exclaim
Remember, dear Sara, you carry our name

Like parents, they'll say, a meaning untrue
But they who begrudge us will judge us all too
Be yourself, my dear don't be like the rest
Whatever you do, always make it your best

And so with much pride, I proudly exclaim
That my child Sara will carry our name

So, my child, you must now know
That my love for you will ever grow
And at that time when I depart
Keep me there within your heart

And yet with much pride, I proudly exclaim
Remember, dear Sara, you carry our name

Wherever you go
And whatever you do
Carry our vast love
Forever with you

And so in this ending, I proudly exclaim
Remember, dear Sara, to cherish our name.

Thank you, dear Sara Rose, who carries my mother's name and the
name of Donna and Joel Levin.

My Daughter in Doggy Clothing

For those who are not dog lovers or are ambivalent about pets of any sort, it is hard for you to understand the role that my Leah played and how she tugs at my heart strings every day and in so many ways. They say a dog is a man's best friend. Leah is everyone's friend, and she has a role for each of us. She even knows our schedules, and there she is watching through the window for her family's arrival. She can't ever read it, but you can and recognize this special creature of God. I do hope that the universe will accommodate her matter as well. She will never die in my heart.

Leah does speak, I'm quite sincere
Each bark a meaning, so very clear
She understands what we do and what we say
Is it time to eat or time for play?
But she has emotions as plain as can be
I know it most assuredly
She watched her grandma so tenderly
And now she does the same for me.

Is there a blessing for this dear creature? Let me find one right now!

This is in the spirit of St. Francis of Assisi and Judaism, believe it or not.

This connection between St. Francis and animals is the single fact about him that most people know. He emphasized that creation includes more than humankind. He always called creatures his brothers and sisters, and he worked to link humans and creatures in the same relationship with God. He in Christianity started the tradition of the blessing of animals. Judaism, long home to blessings of all kinds, also pitched in.

Many synagogues now have their own blessing of the animals, and they say the idea originated in ancient Judaism. Without reference to Francis of Assisi (but occasionally, with a passing reference to him), the Jewish ceremony is often performed on the seventh day of Passover (in the spring) as a celebration of the Hebrews' (and their animals') emancipation from slavery in Egypt (the exodus led by Moses, the Levite). These prayers remind us that a dog is not a slave but a companion. I must tell you that when we were saying the memorial prayers for my dad, my Weimeraner slowly walked into the room. Everybody rushed to kick her out, but the rabbi said, "No, do not do so." And he explained that this was one of her own family, and as a creature of creation, she deserved to be in the room. Heidi glanced up at me and never left my side.

> Blessed are You, Holy Source,
> Maker of all living creatures.
> On the fifth and sixth days of creation,
> you called forth fish in the sea,
> birds in the air and animals on the land.
> You inspired us to call all animals brothers and
> sisters.
> We ask you to bless these animals
> by the power of your love,
> enable them to live fully in praise to your Name
> May we always praise you
> for all your beauty in creation.
> Blessed are You, Lord our God, in all your creatures!

And to my readers and all of my friends:

There is a little background here that I want you to know. My father's mother, Tziryl (Cecilia), whom my daughter is named after, was the daughter of a high priest in Judaism. They, the *Kohanim*, which means priest, were in charge of the temple services. The high priests belonged to the Jewish priestly families that trace their paternal line back to Aaron, the first high priest and the elder brother of Moses. Today, without a temple, their job is to bless the people during special holidays. I ask permission of my great-grandfather to recite this one for you in a moment.

The other interesting thought is that with a name Levin, or if you remember that cumbersome LeVein, are we Levites from the tribe of Levi? I'm not sure. The Levites who were not Kohanim (but the Kohanim were all Levites) played music, wrote poetry in the temple, or served to train priests and other apprentice Levites in their respective roles. Could this be where my talent and love for music came from? I was playing skillfully and reading notes before I could master sentences and paragraphs. If not a Levite, it matters not, as I served my practice and my patients with much devotion. I also poured out my feelings through the music, prose, or poetry, which I have always loved.

Anyhow, be you of any faith or creed, this is the Kohanim blessing I send to you. It is in every Hebrew prayer book for all to see.

May the Lord bless you and protect you:
May the Lord show you kindness and be gracious to you:
May the Lord bestow favor upon you and grant you
peace:
May this be God's will.

From my Irish friends:

> May peace and plenty bless your world
> with joy that long endures.
> May all life's passing seasons
> bring the best to you and yours.

From Native Americans

This one is the most healing for me and I hope for you too. It fits perfectly with my newfound faith. Read this, and you'll see what I mean.

I Give You This One Thought

I give you this one thought to keep: I am with you still—I do not sleep. I am a thousand winds that blow, I am the diamond glints on snow, I am the sunlight on ripened grain, and I am the gentle autumn rain. When you awaken in the morning's hush, I am the swift, uplifting rush of quiet birds in circled flight. I am the soft stars that shine at night. Do not think of me as gone—I am with you still—in each new dawn.

> *And this my wish for you all*
> My beguine has ended, my dance is through
> But as I end, I think of you
> May the curtains rise, the orchestra play
> To bring you the rapture that once came my way

Our memoir is over, in that you can tell
I've told the story in truth as well
May you all live on as you dance to your fate.
And begin your beguine, it's never too late

And as I speak for my soul mate she would say:

My life has ended on this earth
I could no longer stay
God gave me so much time
Then called me on my way

I know my family weeps for me
I feel it in my soul
But cherished thoughts I leave to all
Remember Donna's role

And to my beloved mate in life
Try not to despair
Remember keep me in your heart
That way I'm always there

I played my part, I danced the dance
And life was not so bad
I did love life, and most of all
The children that I had
Good times, good friends, my Joel's touch.
I'm sure there is much sorrow
But I was called, it was my time
There would be no tomorrow

But if he's right and souls are real
And mine is living now
It's possible if you believe
We'll meet again somehow.

This is our story, and this was our journey. Donna was my beguine, and my dance of life started with her. That now is fully clear in my mind after reviewing our life apart and then together. The last premise is will we be together again, somewhere, somehow?

Love from Donna and Joel. We told it as it was meant to be told—like it was with the music of our life and with all our joys and our sorrows. I speak for her, as I know she is near me, helping me write every word, telling our story, smiling her beautiful smile, and believing as I do that we were soul mates destined to have our dance through life together from the start. And as of now, we still share in this vast universe together, and she remains the inspiration for my humble words. Our music now is the music of creation, of stars and angels, of dreams, and of nightly remembrance for the best wife a fella could ever have!

So take care of her where ye Angels abide,
For nee'r more I'll have her at my side.
So keep her safe—so safe for me,
Till all my matter and atoms are free.

Thank you all for reading this memoir. It is a bit unique, as the musician and physician within me had to tell the story in their own way, which when put together became my way.

Fare thee well for now. I hope that this memoir of two people, Donna and Joel, who were clearly destined to be together will bring a measure of peace and a successful closure to those who have unresolved sorrows and mainly inspiration to the rest of you. I hope also that you recognize that letting grief go is not forgetting. I shall never do so. Please, those of you who knew her and loved her, keep her in your thoughts.

Lastly in closing, there is time for all of you to enjoy that which you have and those that you love. That is what I call the dance of life. So, my friends, it is never too late to continue or begin your beguine!

Being in a profound state of shock when Donna died, I was an empty shell and could not express my feelings in front of others. My dear granddaughter did so with great passion for her grandmother at the funeral. I will remember her words always. But now as I said, the pain remains, my loss is great, my heart remains broken; yet I must in this memoir eulogize my wife. The only way I can do so is to turn to my poetry. The prose in life is much more difficult and so complex. We were human with all our faults and frailties. I spoke somewhat about that earlier on. In order to keep the tender thoughts pure, just as her soul is pure, here are my thoughts for my soul mate Donna Joyce Krakow Levin.

My Eulogy

The dance of life began with thee;
That is simply plain to see.
My early life was to prepare
My life to share,
My life to share.

The early dance we call beguine
Was troublefree and so serene.
The Gods of fate did us prepare
Our souls to share,
Our souls to share.

In later times the pleasures grew,
But yet there were some problems too.
The path of life at times did scare,
But you were there,
Yes, you were there.

As life progressed, we did renew;
Our bond of love continued too.
We were bashert from up above
And you my love,
Yes, you my love.

Our life went on, and so we danced;
We laughed and cried, as age advanced.
And laughed it off without prepare
'Cause you were there,
Yes, you were there.

Our dance did slow with body ill,
Began to change our very will.
You smiled, yet dread we dared not share.
We were aware,
But you were there.

Together dancing on our path,
Some days of joy some days of wrath,
We held our hands for all to see.
Yes, I loved you,
And you loved me.

When came that dreaded time for me,
Your illness brought me to my knee.
With all my will, with all my might,
I begged for you, my shining light,
Yes, begged for you, my shining light.

You fought the fight; you fought with dare
All night and day, you in my care.
The beguine now slowed, the dance near end.
I tried my very soul to lend;
Yes, tried my very soul to lend.

I know that you were meant for me,
And so I rushed, my love, to see
The day that ends our destiny.
You waited till I came to thee,
Yes, waited till I came to thee.

Upon your chest my head did rest;
This terrible moment was my test,
For you were gone, so plain to see.
My soul mate lost, no more to be.
My soul mate lost, no more to be.

Today I walk the path alone,
Yet love for you has grown and grown.
Yet thoughts prevailed and troubled me:
Where could you be?
Where could you be?

Today, you lie beneath the earth,
And I in passion know your worth.
It's something that I keep in sight.
You were my light;
You were my light.

And so I searched for hope, you see,
Researched the soul, where could it flee
From this realm to eternity.
Yes, you are free;
Yes, you are free.

I'm finished; the beguine now done.
We had some fun, some battles won.
I think of you from day to night;
You see, my love, you were my light,
Yes, you, my love, a mighty light.

I walk alone; I cry in pain,
But not for me, for you; it's plain.
I ask that heaven play its role
To shelter you, to guard your soul,
Yes, shelter you and guard your soul.

In patience now I tell to all,

Your death upon me was my fall.

Yet newfound hope and science ken

Tells me our souls will meet again.

Oh yes, our souls will meet again.

Till we met again, rest in peace, my darling.

Epilogue

Donna's Four Quarters of Her Life

The Windmills of Your Mind

Like a circle in a spiral, like a wheel within a wheel
Never ending or beginning on an ever-spinning reel
As the images unwind like the circles that you find
In the windmills of your mind

"The Windmills of Your Mind" (Les Moulins de Ton Coeur) is a song with music by French composer Michel Legrand and English lyrics written by Americans Alan Bergman and Marilyn Bergman. The French lyrics, under the title "Les Moulins de Mon Cœur," were written by Eddy Marnay.

As I promised earlier in this memoir, it is time to share Donna's own thoughts, which were like an unleashing of her thought processes, the remembrance of her earlier life and her life to the date she wrote down. I found this at the bottom of her nightstand after she was gone.

It makes me sad but happy to preserve this in our memoir. I think she was journaling at this late date, a little melancholy about age and illness. She called this her four quarters.

I continue to mention that Donna always had a smile throughout her life, but unlike Mona Lisa, she was never cold, though often lonely. It was a mask to hide her broken heart, as well as to express her joys and pleasures. So please, my friends, let me be silent as you listen to her own story. Thank goodness I found this.

This is my story—Donna Joyce Levin—April 13, 2009

74 years old and still going, but slowly!

My, my, my. 75 years old. Donna. How about that! Well, I had a Seder on Thursday and it was so nice. Barb, Marty and Reid Miles came. Rella Silvers came. Joyce Katz was here, as well as Irene Katz, and children, Julie, Murray and David too. It was so good having them here. They are as family because we all really care for each other. Lots of bedtime needed to walk again, but it will come. On our birthday, 12 April, we saw a play, Joseph at the Marriott and dinner at Jimmy's. It was nice. I have divided my life into quarters now.

First quarter—age 1 to 25

Normal growing up stuff except for my dad in the Army for some years, and we moved around. Made some long-lasting friends during my school time. Just an average student—two years of college, work at a mail commercial school, dated very little. Met Joel and married at age

22. Dealt with my mom and breast cancer. Not a good outcome and she died when I was 26.

Second quarter—age 25 to 50

Time spent in Army in Europe with Joel. When I was 26, lived with my dad on Lunt Ave., Joel back in training. Adopted first son Ray when 27 (good times and bad. Who knew he would give us up as parents years later.) Next came Ken 15 months later, and then Cheryl two years later. Busy times, raising kids, and trying to have a life. They experimented with drugs and gave us a lot of grief. But of them all, Cheryl rose above it, and is a good daughter, who gave us a very special granddaughter, Sara. They have lived with us for all of Sara's life. We took a lot of trips and cruises and especially remember the Leichenkos (Harold and Eleanor). Those were special times.

Third-quarter—age 50 to 75

Multiple things—moved to Riverwoods and a new house. I developed severe arthritis problems, so I lost my mobility. Joel had prostate cancer, but thank God is doing very well. Life goes on. Have a wonderful dog, Leah Rachel Levin, who loves the four of us.

Fourth Quarter—75 to ???

I will keep trying to go on although walking, using my body and arms is really hard. Who knows what will come into our lives. Sara keeps me going. I am Bubbe, Bubbles and Bub. I sleep a lot, needlepoint, and try to keep going. I just don't want a long illness way to die.

The family on my side has little do with us and it is their loss as false people I can do without.

The last years—today on April 13, 2009. Only time will tell how long I'll be around.

That was my Donna, always telling it like it is (or was).

Many other times, she would say, "However, it's not over until it's over, they say."

The Soul

Donna's death inspired me to search for more information about the soul. I need to know more about what the soul is to help better understand what it means for her to be my soul mate now that she's gone. In this section, I will explore the various aspects of a soul, including its definition, what scriptures say, what a soul mate is, what other cultures say, and traveling souls.

How many of you remember Peggy Lee? I saw her near the end of her career, and backstage between her musical numbers, she had an oxygen-giving device and was using it. Anyhow, she then knew what she was singing with her hit song "Is That All There Is?" The composers of this song, which is so pertinent to this chapter, are Jerry Lieber and Mike Stoller. It was based on a book called *Disillusionment*.

I related to the song in the sense of Donna's and my own regrets within our lifetime, which yielded both the yin and yang of life, the light and the darkness, the pleasures as well as the travails as we traveled on the road of mortality together. It also made me think that this chance may be our one and only; thus, is that all there is? It is in a sense in opposition to my own thoughts of a soul's immortality. This in its entirety is not only a song but deals with a great deal of metaphysical thinking.

Peggy spoke many lines about regrets and then sang the following:

Is that all there is? Is that all there is?
If that's all there is, then let's keep dancing.
Let's break out the booze and have a ball,
If that's all there is.

Her performance of this song started me thinking about the meaning of life, something that I often took for granted.

Then there is another song that comes into my memory, and for me, if not for all of you, speaks of commitment to one another. This is an old Scottish poem put to music, and it ends with the saying, "I would lay me down and die …"

Maxwelton's braes are bonnie,
Where early fa's the dew,
'Twas there that Annie Laurie
Gi'ed me her promise true.
Gi'ed me her promise true -
Which ne'er forgot will be,
And for bonnie Annie Laurie
I'd lay me down and dee.

I think of this because, in our lifetime, I would do anything for her, and I often thought and hoped that she would survive me. That was not meant to be, and when I think of all the new responsibilities placed upon me and the heavy burden on my daughter, I would not have wished upon her all the paperwork that needed to be done. That is why I emotionally relate to this song. Here is another one that even mentions my dear wife's name.

My Better Half—My Soul Mate—Where Are You?

"Donna," by Richie Valens
I had a girl,
Donna was her name
Since she left me
I've never been the same

(This song was on the back side
of his famous record with "La Bamba.")

I needed to explore this aspect of my relationship with Donna, whom I have called my soul mate. Is it all over? What does her death mean, and what is our connection though one of us is now on a different journey.

What is a soul? It is one of life's great mysteries. Any dictionary would describe it in this manner (my source was the Merriam-Webster Online Dictionary):

1. The nonphysical aspect of a person: the complex of human attributes that manifests as consciousness, thought, feeling, and, regarded as distinct from the physical body

2. Feelings: a person's emotional and moral nature, where the most private thoughts and feelings are hidden

3. The spirit surviving death: in some systems of religious and now scientific communities, a belief that it is the spiritual part of a human being believed to continue to exist after the body dies

But are these the only definitions? There are many dissertations on the soul and particularly on traveling souls that meet over and over again working toward perfection.

Following Aristotle and Avicenna as a philosopher, St. Thomas Aquinas (1225–1274) understood the soul to be the first actuality of the living body. Consequent to this, he distinguished three orders of life: plants, which feed and grow; animals, which add sensation to the operations of plants; and humans, which add intellect to the operations of animals. Concerning the human soul, his theory required that, since the knower becomes what he or she knows, the soul was definitely not of the physical body. Therefore, the soul had an operation that did not rely on a bodily organ and so the soul could subsist without the body. Furthermore, since the rational soul of human beings was a subsistent form and not something made up of matter and form, it could not be destroyed in any manner. This is most interesting, as modern-day scientists are looking at the mystery of from whence it comes and where it goes. What happens when human beings die? Is there a final destination for the soul? These were the questions discussed among four scientists on a video that recently aired on *Through the Wormhole*, hosted by Morgan Freeman on the Science channel. A number of scientists who have also studied consciousness and near-death experiences extensively believe they are close to solving the puzzle, but they continue to vehemently disagree with each other about the solution. And so, for you and me and all seekers of this mystical knowledge, we do not yet have the assurance needed to carry on or resolve the issue.

Looking at the Holy Scriptures, we see the word *soul* can refer to both the immaterial and material aspects of humanity. In its most basic sense, the word *soul* means "life." However, beyond this essential meaning, the Bible speaks of the soul in many contexts. The life principle of the soul is removed at the time of physical death (Genesis 35:18; Jeremiah 15:2). The soul, as with the spirit, is the center of many spiritual and emotional experiences (Job 30:25; Psalm 43:5; Jeremiah 13:17). Whenever the word *soul* is used, it can refer to the whole person, whether alive or in the afterlife. The soul and the spirit are connected but separable (Hebrews 4:12). The soul is the essence of humanity's being; it is who we are. The spirit is the aspect of humanity that connects us with God.

Christof Koch, the chief scientific officer of the Allen Institute of Brain Science and the Lois and Victor Troendle Professor of Cognitive and Behavioral Biology at California Institute of Technology, argued that the soul dies and everything is lost when human beings lose consciousness. "You lose everything. The world does not exist anymore for you. Your friends don't exist anymore. You don't exist. Everything is lost," he said. I hope not, say I.

Bruce Greyson, professor of psychiatry at the University of Virginia, challenged Koch's view of consciousness. He said that, "If you take these near death experiences at face value, then they suggest that the mind or the consciousness seems to function without the physical body."

Stuart Hameroff, who proposed the highly controversial Orch-OR (orchestrated objective reduction) theory of consciousness in 1996, along with Roger Penrose, told the Science channel, "I think the quantum approach to consciousness can, in principle, explain why we're here and what our purpose is, and also the possibility of life after death, reincarnation and persistence of consciousness after our bodies give up." I will speak of his theory later on.

Finally, Eben Alexander, who wrote the widely circulated and criticized cover story for *Newsweek*, "Proof of Heaven," said, "I have great belief and knowledge that there is a wonderful existence for our souls outside of this earthly realm and that is our true reality, and we all find that out when we leave this earth. This is a wonderful book that I recommend to all who seek for solace and understanding.

During my very acute period of grief, my friend Irene gave me a book called *Healing after Loss: Daily Meditations for Working through Grief.* The author is Martha Whitmore Hickman. She had lost a daughter when she took up the project of writing this book. I would recommend it to those who have felt the loss of a loved one. It is a day-by-day book filled with her insight and ability to put into writing what most people can't express. It raised many questions in my mind and gave me some solace but still left a huge gap of remorse, sadness, and depression.

Is that how life ends—just physically when one is worn out or organs fail or a dreaded disease occurs. I want so badly to believe that the spiritual part of her remains somewhere in the cosmos. This chapter then has to explore the nonphysical part of being. Using a philosophical thought process, when hearing the common term *heart and soul*, it immediately eliminates in my mind that the heart is the soul. It is an organ; it pumps our blood daily until it wears out. It is real, and it dies with the body. The term *body and soul* seems to define a distinct difference or separation.

And so I search for the meaning of the soul, not as a philosopher, not as a scientist or authority and knowing nothing about quantum mechanics or molecular existence when the body dies. I merely search and think as a humble man, a husband who has had tragedy strike me down. I just know that in my great loss, something that was a part of me was also lost, from the time we first met, and as I believe, the time that we were meant to be. So in my very own way, I have pondered a lot and researched for definitions, interpretations, and meanings that may lessen my loss. I am as an empty shell right now, a part of a grand togetherness with my soul mate, a lonely soul now no longer filled with zest for life, hope, or desire. I just do, exist, and live it day by day. Kindly bear with me as I need to go through this healing process. If it is too heavy a subject, you have my permission to take what you can from it, relate it to your own belief structure, and leave the rest behind.

Definition of Soul Mate

Because Donna is my soul mate, let's start with that definition. A soul mate is a person ideally suited to another as a close friend or romantic partner. This may not be enough in terms of my idea of my soul mate. A closer definition for me is as follows.

A soul mate is a person with whom you have an immediate connection the moment you meet—a connection so strong that you are drawn to that person in a way you have never experienced before. That was so true, as you have seen in my memoir. As this connection develops over time, you experience a love so deep, strong, and complex that you begin to doubt that you have ever truly loved anyone prior. Again, all relationships prior to Donna were frivolous. She connected with me on every level, bringing a sense of peace, calmness, and happiness for the most part.

Neither of us being saints, there were discordant moments in our life, and the music of our life could be harsh. But now not being near her, I am keenly aware of the harshness of life without her. I also remember the beauty in my life. I was given a great gift and will always be thankful for it. My friend Marty will like this definition, and Marty knows why. The American writer Richard Bach said, "A soulmate is someone who has locks that fit our keys, and keys to fit our locks." Oh well, the secret is out. Among his many talents, being a locksmith was one.

The concept of a soul is one humanity has wondered about. It is even in our language. Here are the many ways we all use *soul* in our languages, often erroneously.

- I won't tell it to a soul (a person).

- I won't bare my soul (trust someone with my thoughts or problems).

- I won't tell a soul (again a person).

- Every living soul (This may critical—does the soul live, and where does it reside?)

- Keeping my body and soul together (survival)

- God rest someone's soul. (When someone dies, does God reclaim the soul?)

- Not a living soul (person again)

- Pour out one's soul (an emotional expression)

- Without a soul (lack of compassion)

- Soul searching (self-searching, looking inside, taking inventory of oneself)

So we come to a definition of a soul; as found in any dictionary, *soul* is defined as the spirit and essence of a person.

An example of your soul is that part of you that makes you who you are and that will live on after your death. (This is to my liking!)

An example of soul is the part of you that will go to heaven and be immortal, according to the teachings of certain religions. That may be difficult for nonbelievers or agnostics.

I am not alone in trying to define a soul. Many cultures have also tried. Among the Shoshone, there are three kinds of souls. The first of these is the *ego-soul*, which is embodied in the breath. The second is the *free-soul* that is able to leave the body during dreams, trances, and comas. I think Shirley McClain speaks of this. It is the free soul that encounters the guardian spirit that becomes one's ally during life. Finally, there is the *body-soul*, which activates the body during the waking hours.

The doctrine of reincarnation and many lives is a central tenet of the Indian religions. It is also a common belief of various ancient and modern religions, such as found in many tribal societies around the world, in places such as Siberia, West Africa, North America, and Australia.

Within the Abrahamic religions of Judaism, Christianity, and Islam, fundamental believers do not believe that individuals reincarnate, but particular groups within these religions do refer to reincarnation. Let me refer to the Kabbalah. There is a tradition in Judaism that one must be old enough to begin to understand Jewish mysticism. That I am, but I think of Christians as well, notably the singer Madonna and Hillary Clinton and others who have adopted this and are even still wearing kabbalah bracelets. The red string bracelet is usually made from thin scarlet wool thread. It is worn as a bracelet or band on the left wrist of the wearer (understood in some Kabbalistic theory as the receiving side of the spiritual body). It is knotted seven times and then sanctified with Hebrew blessings. I like that because I am left-handed, Donna was left-handed, and the saying goes, left-handed people think with the right side of their brain.

What am I searching for? Obviously the meaning of life in the now and in a larger sense, the here and now has become critical to me. And so in my search of kabbalistic thinking, the body is seen as an outward cloak for the soul, holder of the spark of divinity within. In the North American native cultures, the shamans were soul seekers, and they employed soul catchers as well. We often called older cultures pagan, but they may have had a level of consciousness and understanding beyond ours. When the Bible says that a human is created in the image of God, it refers to the fact that each human being is like a blueprint of all existence. All souls before birth are originally a composite of male and female, and it is only in their descent to earth that the souls separate into masculine and feminine. Marriage relations are the restoration of the soul that was split at birth. This brings me so much closer to my search for acceptance and peace of mind. It also matches my own definition of bashert/kismet/soul mate, as I explained earlier.

The above examples then that your soul is the part of you that makes you who you are and that will live on after your death are most acceptable to me, as I long to know that this is true. So the soul then escapes death, and I earnestly want to believe that is so for my Donna. William Penn said that they who love beyond the world cannot be separated by it. Death is but crossing the world, as friends do the sea. They live in one another still.

Traveling Souls

Edgar Cayce believed that from the beginning, our souls have tended to travel together in groups, and the very act of traveling together for such long periods creates forces of attraction that help to maintain and build on these group relationships. Nearly all souls on the planet today were together in past ages of human history. As a result, the relationships among the peoples of the world today are a reflection of their past activities with each other.

I think also of people I have seen in my medical practice who with near-death experiences speak of tunnels, of bright lights, of seeing loved ones, and the feeling of sadness on returning to life.

Soul groups are not always in the same relationship. Any individual soul can use its free will to seek an experience in another group. There are many cases of souls changing race, gender, or religion from one lifetime to another. A member of one generation may enter again with another generation. For example, two members of a family group who were father and son in one life may change positions and become son and father in another or a mother become the child. They may even choose not to be in the same generation. There is also a belief structure that each reincarnation is necessary to free oneself from errors in a previous life and to approach what may be called nirvana. This brings up a recollection from my early days as a youth before my mind became so cluttered. In a repetitive dream, I saw myself on a cable car (and I never had seen or heard of one in my life) when it smashed to the ground and my life ended. The only cars I knew in those days were my relatives' personal automobiles and the street car. Do those of you in my age group remember the fun of flattening a coin beneath the street car and its tracks? It's not as much fun today when there are machines in museums that will produce a piece of memorabilia for you, if you pay for it, of course.

Anyhow, Wordsworth's *Ode: Intimations of Immortality from Recollections of Early Childhood* corroborates that humans have altruistic instincts (which Wordsworth equates with a "heavenly" state), which are then later buried by our consciousness.

> Our birth is but a sleep and a forgetting:
> The Soul that rises with us, our life's Star,
> Hath had elsewhere its setting,
> And cometh from afar …

This suggests that heaven is the birth of our infancy (or being born again?).

A Prayer

On the anniversary of Donna's death when I kindle a flame in a lamp or within my heart in remembrance of her now completed dance of life, there is a prayer that speaks of the soul. The teaching is that human souls are the candles that bring light to the world (we all have within us the sparks of the highest power). We are as microcosms of a creator or creating force, whichever concept one wishes to believe, each in our own way. I have always been an agnostic being as a physician. There was always a need to prove a theory or to be sure of the treatment that you rendered. On the other hand, as a musician, the emotional and open side of me wants to believe without a doubt that there is more beyond this existence.

Somehow, as a child, I remember this prayer and seem to think my mother taught it to me and I said this for several years. It, to me, is another bit of proof that the soul is separate from the body and in the care of a higher power. There was an older version and a later one, which I would like to repeat for you. Perhaps the earliest version was written by Joseph Addison in an essay appearing in the *Spectator* on March 8, 1711. A later version printed in the *New England Primer* goes:

> Now I lay me down to sleep,
> I pray the Lord my soul to keep,
> If I shall die before I wake,
> I pray the Lord my soul to take.

Does Science Have an Answer to the Soul and the Cosmos?

This is perhaps the most exciting or interesting part of our discussion. Can science define the soul and where it comes to lie in wait for yet another journey?

This is mind-boggling but, importantly, for me, begs the question of whether humans and other living creatures have souls. As Kant pointed out over two hundred years ago, everything we experience—including all the colors, sensations, and objects we perceive—is nothing but representation in our minds. Space and time are simply the mind's tools for putting it all together. Scientists are beginning dimly to recognize that those rules make existence itself possible. Indeed, the experiments above suggest that objects only exist with real properties if they are observed. The results suggest that a part of the mind—the soul—is immortal and exists outside of space and time.

"The hope of another life," wrote Will Durant, "gives us courage to meet our own death, and to bear with the death of our loved ones; we are twice armed if we fight with faith."

And are we further armed if we ally ourselves not with religious or spiritual belief but with science?

Life and consciousness are central to this new scientific view of being, reality, and the cosmos. Although the current scientific paradigm is based on the belief that the world has an objective observer-independent existence, real experiments suggest just the opposite. We think life is just the activity of atoms and particles, which spin around for a while and then dissipate into nothingness (death). If we but add life to the equation, we may change our thinking about the universe. While neuroscience has made tremendous progress illuminating the functioning of the brain, why we have subjective experiences remains mysterious. The problem of the soul lies exactly here, in understanding the nature of the self, which lives and emotionally feels life. This isn't just a problem for biology and cognitive science, but for the whole of Western natural philosophy itself. So then, the mind as the heart is not the bearer of the soul. The Bible, by the way, speaks of other worlds, other planets, and other realms of consciousness. Is science going to be able to prove it?

Consider the famous two-slit experiment. Some scientists doing this experiment say that when you watch a particle go through the holes, it behaves like a bullet, passing through one slit or the other. But if no one observes the particle, it exhibits the behavior of a wave and can pass through both slits at the same time. This and other experiments tell us that unobserved particles exist only as "waves of probability" as the great Nobel laureate Max Born demonstrated in 1926. They're statistical predictions—nothing but a likely outcome. Until observed, they have no real existence; only when the mind sets the process in place can they be thought of as having duration or a position in space.

Science states and has proved that energy in motion stays in motion. That is all life is—energy. And therefore, one must believe that our energy "stays in motion" in accordance with the laws of physics.

In a video that recently aired on *Through the Wormhole*, narrated by Morgan Freeman on the TV channel Science, Dr. Hameroff claims, "I believe that consciousness, or its immediate precursor proto-consciousness, has been in the universe all along, perhaps from the Big Bang." I watched it with fascination. I don't understand it, but Dr. Stuart Hameroff, MD, professor emeritus at the Departments of Anesthesiology and Psychology and the director of the Center of Consciousness Studies at the University of Arizona over the past few decades has done research in the field of quantum mechanics, dedicated to studying consciousness. He and Roger Penrose, mathematician and physicist, proposed that consciousness is derived from microtubules within brain cells (neurons), which are sites of quantum processing.

For example, according to Dr. Hameroff, in a near-death experience, when the heart stops beating, the blood stops flowing, and the microtubules within our brain lose their quantum state, but the quantum information in the microtubules isn't destroyed. It's distributed to the universe at large, and if the patient is revived, the quantum information can go back to the microtubules. In this event, the patient says he or she had something like a near-death experience, i.e., saw white light or a tunnel or floated out of his or her body. In the event that the patient is not revived, "It's possible that the quantum information can exist outside the body, perhaps indefinitely, as a soul. Thus it is held that our souls are more than the interaction of neurons in the brain. They are in fact constructed from the very fabric of the universe—and may have existed since the beginning of time."

That is about all I can fathom or understand, but it gives me, the agnostic one and a physician/musician duality, a glimmer of hope and joy that my loved one is yet part of the greater universe. I cannot touch her or see her, of course, but if her soul is where angels dwell, there is some comfort for my saddened mind. It seems to me that we are approaching an era where science and religion are one and the same, yet coming at the issue of the soul from opposing vantage points—from a belief system as in religion or an experimental one on the scientific side.

I want to believe that Donna may not physically exist but her life's energy does. Oh how I wish I could connect with it. Sometimes, I can through the poetry, emotion, and spirit that lingers within my soul. Our beguine is over, but perhaps we will somehow meet again, unknowingly, for sure. Everywhere that I go, every stranger I see, I look to see if there is someone, perhaps a newborn child or a young person who lights up that spark in me. Alas, that has not happened.

This period of my life is intense and sorrowful. They call it bereavement. I was given a lot of advice on how best to cope. I was told to write my thoughts down, which led me to this huge undertaking of memoir and soul searching. I was told to journal a lot in order to lessen some of my sorrow, to mediate, and to surround myself with her photographs and her works of art. I did so and hired an art consultant to place many of her wondrous works on the walls of our home. When I see them—the beautiful ladies she created and the wondrous mixture of threads and colors that she used—it leads to moments of reflection and a form of peaceful meditation. They are no substitute for her but for me remain a connection to my soul mate and the place she occupied in my heart.

Other than the writing of this book, I remained in a deep state of mourning. I saw a psychologist for a while who recommended that I attend a bereavement group. Having had the experience with self-help groups earlier in life, this did not intimidate me.

Searching around, I found the Cancer Wellness Center in Northbrook, Illinois, and was contacted by a very caring bereavement program coordinator. We made arrangements for me to join one of her groups. I soon began to see that my grief was a process shared by the group members and that the physical as well as emotional changes within me were quite normal. It helped me understand my anger at her physicians, my anger that Donna left me, and my frequent outbursts of intense grief that appear without warning and lead me downward into a sinkhole of depression and crying.

I was instructed as to my rights to grieve in my own manner and time and crying, which I do often, is okay. I noticed that I had become silent at times with family and friends, refusing invitations, abhorring holidays and anniversaries, and this too was my own right.

When meeting with my new friends and our coordinator, I learned to share my story with the others and respectfully listen to them, never giving advice but intently listening to our shared experiences. The meetings have resulted in some early changes where I dare to meet with family and friends and avoid the "third wheel" feeling when I meet with couples Donna and I knew over the years.

We were given a handout at the first meeting, and I would like to share it with you.

Falling Apart
By Eloise Cole

I seem to be falling apart
My attention span can be measured in seconds
I am normal I am told
I am a newly grieving person

Used with permission (1985) by Eloise Cole, Scottsdale,
Arizona

Some of this is quite accurate, but I am blessed by our daughter who does whatever she can to keep our home fires burning.

We have talked about the soul in religious, esoteric, and scientific ways. Within my current life, I can objectively illustrate this for the reader in a more direct way. One's life has to have a balance between work and other life duties or pleasures. My life has been unbalanced since Donna died. Many of my efforts to keep myself free from depression have been to occupy my time with my profession and my job.

As mentioned, I have wonderful family and friends who love me and support me in different ways. I thank them all for that. I have a bereavement group that I attend, and a lot of empathy and support occurs at these meetings.

You would think that the workplace could be an area where things are professional and deal only with medical matters. I can listen and show empathy for my patients; however, the reverse does not occur.

A mystical thing though has happened in my daily work, which to me is a concrete example of a special empathy and understanding from afar. I have never met or seen this person I speak of, but I deal professionally with her every day. She lives in one state and I in another. Of all the wonderful people in our national company, I had an uncanny feeling that I could trust her with my feelings and had a strong desire to do so. Is it because she is goodhearted, which I know she is? I think there is another reason. For some reason I have an uncanny feeling that I know her in a deeper sense. People call this a kindred spirit.

The definition of a kindred spirit is a person who shares beliefs, attitudes, feelings, or features with another—also called a kindred soul! (Dictionary.com, 21st Century Lexicon, © 2003–2014, Dictionary. com, LLC)

To me this is an uncanny and lucky stroke for me, or is it luck? Was it meant to be? Is it an example of the traveling souls that Edgar Cayce spoke of? I don't know the answer, but there is a deep feeling within me that there is more than this one plane of existence. I will end this line of thinking with a poem that has swept into my heart.

A Friend of Worth

The road of life, when youth doth harken,
Knowing not the path will darken,
Grief and loss will take away
The pleasant thoughts of yesterday.

So on and on the path gets rougher;
Alone, your very soul doth suffer,
Looking o'er each troubled bend

For someone who can be a friend.

Friends arrive but slowly part;
Condolence is a special art.
Empathy, for some, a mere cliché;
Healing words are not their way.

Travails of life now seem much rougher;
Mind and matter both do suffer
Thoughts of life without my mate,
Wistful fears of my own fate.

By chance one day, the path did brighten;
At last, I prayed—could life now lighten,
With pleasures none and woes immense?
Was this false hope, a mere pretense?

I have this job, which brought me pleasure,
But through the gods of fate, a treasure.
I knew her not, her face unknown,
Yet there was something in her tone.

At last, thought I—a special kind
Whose heart and soul could clear my mind,
Who understood my shattered life.
In trust, I shared my inner strife.

She listened in a special way,
Knowing what to do or say.
I bared my soul to one, with fear;

Yet afar, she seemed so near.

Upon life's road I found a friend
Who really cared, did not pretend,
Who daily when we did converse
Could with her words my fears reverse.

A heart and soul can reach your mind
With demeanor of a special kind.
This friend afar has helped me through
My darkened road, somehow she knew.

Never would I take the dare
To bare my soul without a care;
My road so rough, each day a trial,
Yet from a distance came a smile.

In ending this I do remind
That there are those of humankind
Who rise above and bring forth cheer
To those in need, to ease their fear.

My mind can rest because she cared
And listened daily as I dared.
To sum it up now as I end,
Indeed she is a special friend.

Let me end this section on bereavement and the concepts of the soul by quoting Psalm 23:4–6. It speaks of the departed one, but make no mistake; Donna did not walk through that valley alone. I walked with her, and her daughter and granddaughter walked with her every day, sitting at the bedside, holding hands, caretaking, and always sharing the fears and anguish of the situation.

> Even though I walk through the valley of the shadow of death, I fear no evil: for thou art with me; thy rod and thy staff, they comfort me. Thou preparest a table before me in the presence of mine enemies; thou anointest my head with oil, my cup overflows. Surely goodness and mercy shall follow me all the days of my life; and I shall dwell in the house of the lord forever (Psalm 23:4–6).

It gives me comfort, for I believe her soul remains a shining light in her new existence, just as the physical Donna did through her lifetime for me. As the song "You Light Up My Life" states, you gave me strength to carry on. You were the light of my life. I shall know no other.

CPSIA information can be obtained at www.ICGtesting.com
Printed in the USA
LVOW07s0512020415

432927LV00001B/5/P